ASIAN

Ralph Johnson
First Baptist Church
Oak, Park, Illinois
5/19/67

The

HOLY SPIRIT

The
HOLY SPIRIT

By
CHARLES CALDWELL RYRIE

MOODY PRESS
CHICAGO

CONTENTS

INTRODUCTION

Spiritual power! What pictures and hopes that brings before the believer's mind! And it is right that it should, for spiritual power is the proper longing of God's people.

However Christians may differ on the means to spiritual power, all agree that it is the work of the Holy Spirit. No subject, therefore, could be of greater significance to the child of God than that of the Holy Spirit. A Christian is one who has received Jesus Christ; a spiritual Christian is one who displays Christ living through his life, and this is done by the power of the indwelling Holy Spirit.

Spirituality, then, is Christlikeness, and Christlikeness is the fruit of the Spirit. What better portrait of Jesus Christ is there than "love, joy, peace, long-suffering, gentleness, goodness, faithfulness, meekness, self-control"? This is the fruit of the Spirit. Spiritual power is not necessarily or usually the miraculous or spectacular but rather the consistent exhibition of the characteristics of the Lord Jesus in the believer's life. All of this is the work of the Holy Spirit, of whom the Lord Jesus said, "He shall glorify me."

An understanding of the ministry of the Holy Spirit is basic to Christian living. But one cannot fully comprehend the work of a person without also knowing something about that person. Likewise it is necessary to know something about the person of the Holy Spirit in order to appreciate fully His work. It may seem dull to the reader to pursue the study of the Spirit's personality and deity; but what He is is vital to what He does, and a knowledge of both His person and work is basic to Christian devotion and living.

No other portion of the family of God has ever received so many of the ministries of the Spirit as has the Church of God since Pentecost. His permanent indwelling of every believer was not experienced before. His work of joining believers to the risen

Christ was impossible before the resurrection of Christ and the descent of the Spirit at Pentecost. His teaching ministry, His comfort, His intercession are benefits that all Christians may experience without restriction today. This is truly the age of the Spirit, and none of the people of God have been as greatly privileged as are Christians in this age.

Paul wrote only one circular letter to a group of churches and that was Ephesians, which was sent to all the churches in Asia Minor. It is interesting to notice how frequently he mentions various ministries of the Holy Spirit in this epistle. It is as if the Spirit were a wide-spectrum antibiotic for the ills of the people. Paul reminded those who might lack assurance of their salvation that the Spirit had sealed them and that His presence in their lives was the earnest or guarantee of the everlasting character of their redemption (Eph. 1:13-14). If God has put His own seal of ownership upon us in the person of His Spirit, then nothing could be more secure than our redemption. The seemingly impossible work of uniting Jews and Gentiles in one body was accomplished by the Spirit, and this union brings with it an access or introduction into the very presence of the Father (Eph. 2:18). Paul assures those who need strength to let Christ reign in their lives that the Holy Spirit will give it (Eph. 3:16), and when He does, they can begin to understand the dimensions of the love of Christ, for "he shall glorify me."

The very practical and important problem of relationships to other believers is to be guided and guarded by the principle of "endeavoring to keep the unity of the Spirit in the bond of peace" (Eph. 4:3). One body, one Spirit, one hope, one Lord, one faith, one baptism, and one God are the bases for this principle of unity. The reason for disunity is sin, and one of the gravest sins is the misuse of the tongue; so Paul reminded his readers that useless speech (to say nothing of sinful speech) grieves the Holy Spirit (Eph. 4:29-31). The Spirit's presence in our lives should set a guard over our tongues. The offensive weapons in the believer's armor are the sword of the Spirit and prayer in the Spirit (Eph. 6:17-18). The way to spiritual power is to be filled with the Spirit, which simply means to be controlled by the Spirit (Eph. 5:18). The Holy Spirit in the individual life and in the corporate life of the church is really a theme of this circular letter we call Ephesians.

The solution to the problems of the church today is to solve the individual Christian's problems, and the solution to those problems is a Person—the Holy Spirit. He is the antidote for every error, the power for every weakness, the victory for every defeat, and the answer for every need. And He is available to every believer, for He lives in his heart and life. The answer and the power have already been given us in the indwelling Holy Spirit.

A few summers ago I was about to leave home for three consecutive weeks of camps and conferences when I came down with laryngitis. In desperation I went to the doctor, seeking some miracle cure that would enable me to keep all the speaking commitments involved in those three weeks. He simply told me to go home, go to bed, and drink large quantities of liquid. But this did not satisfy me. I thought he really wasn't doing his job well because he had not prescribed some powerful medicine. At my insistence he at last did give me some very expensive and supposedly powerful pills. But he added that the rest and forcing of fluids would do more than the medicine.

But I really did not believe him. At least I did not act like it, for I faithfully took the pills every four hours to the minute. But the only extra water I drank was that which was required to help swallow the pills. So every four hours I had two extra swallows of water. Somehow I did recover, but it was in spite of my conduct, not because of it.

If this were a book that offered you some new and startlingly different formula for spiritual power, I am sure the sales of it would be phenomenal. You would probably devour its contents at one sitting. This is not that kind of book, for there is no new and startlingly different formula for spiritual power. There can be nothing new or more added to that which God has already provided, for He has given us His Holy Spirit to live within. He is as available as water, and there is no need for expensive pills or programs in addition. But the pity is that most Christians act as I did when I had laryngitis. We look for the new, the miraculous, the secret formula, and we completely overlook the water that is freely available. We flock after the preacher who has some new secret for victory, and we ignore the Holy Spirit who has been freely given to us and who wants to overflow our lives. We do not need to have more of Him, but we do desperately need to know more of Him, and with the increased knowledge will come added faith, power, and control in our lives.

For that purpose this outline study has been written. May its use produce in its readers increased knowledge of the Holy Spirit, complete yieldedness to His control, and full experience of His many ministries, to the end that the living Lord Jesus Christ will be exhibited in every life. When this is done, then we can know that we have learned well the doctrine of the Holy Spirit.

1

THE PERSONALITY OF THE
HOLY SPIRIT

THE TRUTH of the personality of the Holy Spirit is of fundamental importance. To deny it is to deny His real existence, the existence of the Trinity, and the teaching of the Scriptures on the subject. Nevertheless, His personality has been denied throughout the ages, first by the Monarchians, the Arians (Arius called Him the "exerted energy of God"), and the Socinians in the days of the Reformation. In more recent times His personality has been denied by Schleiermacher, Ritschl, the Unitarians, liberals, and by almost all neoorthodox theologians (see Chapter 19 on history). Often those who deny His distinct personality substitute the word *personification* for *personality,* but it does not have the same meaning in their teaching as personality does in orthodox doctrine.

I. THE REASONS FOR THE DOCTRINE
OF PERSONALITY

A. The Holy Spirit Has the *Attributes* of Personality

If personality may be simply defined as possessing intellect, emotions or sensibility, and will, then it may be easily demonstrated that the Holy Spirit has personality because He has intelligence, emotions, and a will.

1. *Intellect.* The Holy Spirit knows and searches the things of God (I Cor. 2:10-11; cf. Isa. 11:2; Eph. 1:17). He is said to possess a mind (Rom. 8:27) and to be able to teach men (I Cor. 2:13).

2. *Emotions or sensibility.* The fact that the Scriptures show that the Holy Spirit has feelings is a further proof of His personality. For instance, it is said that the Spirit can be grieved by the sinful actions of believers (Eph. 4:30—"And grieve not the holy Spirit of God, whereby ye are sealed unto the day of redemption"), a fact which would be meaningless if He were not a person (for an influence cannot be grieved). In another place

11

Paul bases an exhortation on the "love of the Spirit" (Rom. 15:30).

3. *Will.* The distribution of spiritual gifts is said to be according to the will of the Spirit (I Cor. 12:11), and He is able to direct the activities of God's servants. This is well illustrated by the Spirit's leading Paul at Mysia and Troas. He forbade Paul to preach in Asia and Bithynia, and then led him and his party to Europe through the vision of the man of Macedonia (Acts 16:6-11).

In addition to these particulars, the entire doctrine of the deity of the Spirit is further proof of His personality (as explained in Chapter 2).

B. He Performs the *Actions* of Personality

Actions are attributed to the Holy Spirit which cannot be attributed to a mere thing or influence or power or emanation. Such actions, then, must be those of a person, thus proving personality of the Spirit.

1. *The Spirit teaches*—"But the Comforter, which is the Holy Ghost, whom the Father will send in my name, he shall teach you all things, and bring all things to your remembrance, whatsoever I have said unto you" (John 14:26).

2. *The Spirit testifies or witnesses*—"But when the Comforter is come, whom I will send unto you from the Father, even the Spirit of truth, which proceedeth from the Father, he shall testify of me" (John 15:26); "The Spirit itself [himself] beareth witness with our spirit, that we are the children of God" (Rom. 8:16).

3. *The Spirit guides*—"For as many as are led by the Spirit of God, they are the sons of God" (Rom. 8:14).

4. *The Spirit convinces*—"Nevertheless I tell you the truth; it is expedient for you that I go away: for if I go not away, the Comforter will not come unto you; but if I depart, I will send him unto you. And when he is come, he will reprove the world of sin, and of righteousness, and of judgment" (John 16:7-8).

5. *The Spirit restrains*—"And the Lord said, My spirit shall not always strive with man, for that he also is flesh: yet his days shall be an hundred and twenty years" (Gen. 6:3).

6. *The Spirit commands and directs people*—"Then the Spirit said unto Philip, Go near, and join thyself to this chariot" (Acts 8:29).

7. *The Spirit performs miracles*—"And when they were come up out of the water, the Spirit of the Lord caught away Philip, that the eunuch saw him no more: and he went on his way rejoicing" (Acts 8:39).

8. *The Spirit calls for special service*—"As they ministered to the Lord, and fasted, the Holy Ghost said, Separate me Barnabas and Saul for the work whereunto I have called them" (Acts 13:2).

9. *The Spirit sends forth into Christian service*—"So they, being sent forth by the Holy Ghost, departed unto Seleucia; and from thence they sailed to Cyprus" (Acts 13:4).

10. *The Spirit intercedes*—"Likewise the Spirit also helpeth our infirmities: for we know not what we should pray for as we ought: but the Spirit itself [himself] maketh intercession for us with groanings which cannot be uttered" (Rom. 8:26).

These are not actions which could be performed by an impersonal something but only by a personal being.

C. He Receives the *Ascriptions* of Personality

Certain acts are performed toward the Holy Spirit which would be most incongruous if He did not possess true personality.

1. *The Spirit can be obeyed*—"While Peter thought on the vision, the Spirit said unto him, Behold, three men seek thee. Arise therefore, and get thee down, and go with them, doubting nothing: for I have sent them. Then Peter went down to the men which were sent unto him from Cornelius" (Acts 10:19-21a).

2. *The Spirit can be lied to*—"But Peter said, Ananias, why hath Satan filled thine heart to lie to the Holy Ghost, and to keep back part of the price of the land?" (Acts 5:3).

3. *The Spirit can be resisted*—"Ye stiffnecked and uncircumcised in heart and ears, ye do always resist the Holy Ghost: as your fathers did, so do ye" (Acts 7:51).

4. *The Spirit can be grieved*—"And grieve not the holy Spirit of God, whereby ye are sealed unto the day of redemption" (Eph. 4:30).

5. *The Spirit can be reverenced*—"Cast me not away from thy presence; and take not thy holy spirit from me" (Ps. 51:11).

6. *The Spirit can be blasphemed*—"Wherefore I say unto you, All manner of sin and blasphemy shall be forgiven unto men: but the blasphemy against the Holy Ghost shall not be forgiven unto men" (Matt. 12:31).

7. *The Spirit can be outraged*—"Of how much sorer punishment, suppose ye, shall he be thought worthy, who hath trodden under foot the Son of God, and hath counted the blood of the covenant, wherewith he was sanctified, an unholy thing, and hath done despite unto the Spirit of grace?" (Heb. 10:29).

As stated, to act in these various ways toward an influence would be unheard of. These acts therefore ascribe personality to the one toward whom they are performed, the Holy Spirit.

D. He Contradicts the *Accidence* of Personality (Accidence—"the rudiments of grammar")

The Greek word for spirit is *pneuma* (from which we derive English words that have to do with air, like "pneumatic" and "pneumonia") and is a neuter gender word. According to every normal rule of grammar, any pronoun that would be substituted for this neuter noun would itself have to be neuter. However, in several places the biblical writers did not follow this normal procedure of grammar, and instead of using a neuter pronoun in place of the neuter noun *pneuma*, they deliberately contradicted the grammatical rule and used masculine pronouns. Indeed, they used three different kinds of pronouns, all in the masculine gender. This shows that they considered the Spirit to be a person and not merely a thing.

1. In John 16:13-14 the masculine demonstrative pronoun is used for *pneuma*. (Demonstrative pronouns are "this" and "that.") The same demonstrative pronoun is found twice in these verses, once in verse 13 ("howbeit when *he*") and once in verse 14 (*"he* shall glorify me"). Instead of "he," the translation would better be "that person" in these two instances.

2. In John 15:26 and Ephesians 1:14 the masculine relative pronoun is used for the neuter noun *pneuma*, Spirit. (Relative pronouns are translated "who" if masculine or feminine, and "which" if neuter.) In John 15:26 the masculine relative pronoun is the "whom" in the phrase "whom I will send unto you from the Father." In Ephesians 1:14 the masculine pronoun (in the Greek) is the first word in the verse—"which is the earnest of our inheritance until the redemption of the purchased possession, unto the praise of his glory."

3. In John 16:7-8 the masculine personal pronoun is used in place of the neuter noun for Spirit. (The masculine personal

pronoun is "he"; the feminine, "she"; the neuter, "it.") ". . . but if I depart, I will send *him* unto you."

These departures from the normal rules of grammar in connection with the use of several kinds of pronouns are significant proofs of the real personality of the Holy Spirit.

II. THE RAMIFICATIONS OF THE DOCTRINE OF PERSONALITY

A. In Relation to the Idea of Personality

Those who argue against the personality of the Holy Spirit often err in their basic definition of personality. They define it by what is known of human personality, but all human personality is imperfect. God alone has perfect personality, so any definition of true personality must start from a study of God's characteristics. Usually those who deny the personality of the Holy Spirit do not deny the personality of God the Father and sometimes do not deny that of the Son either. Therefore, if the Holy Spirit is shown to be God, then it has also been demonstrated that the Holy Spirit has personality according to the God-oriented definition of personality. It is a false assumption to suppose that perfect personality exists in any human being. Of course, it goes without saying that true personality need not necessarily involve corporeality (possessing a physical body). For example, when people die they do not cease to be persons even though they no longer possess physical bodies.

B. In Relation to Other Persons

If the Holy Spirit has personality, then one would expect to find Him related to other persons as a separate and identifiable personality. Such is the case in the following examples:

1. He is related to the apostles as if He has personality just as they do. At the same time He is distinguished from them as a separate person. "For it seemed good to the Holy Ghost, and to us, to lay upon you no greater burden than these necessary things" (Acts 15:28). It would seem quite unnatural thus to associate Him with the apostles if He were a mere influence or force.

2. He is related to the Lord Jesus Christ in such a way that if the Lord has personality it must be concluded that the Spirit does too. At the same time the Spirit is distinguished from Christ

so that we know that they are not the same person. "He shall glorify me: for he shall receive of mine, and shall show it unto you" (John 16:14).

3. The Holy Spirit is also related to both of the other persons of the Trinity in such a way as to indicate personality. In the passages where this occurs it would be completely unnatural to regard the Spirit as a thing while understanding the Father and the Son as persons. The baptismal formula is in the "name of the Father, and of the Son, and of the Holy Ghost" (Matt. 28:19). Not only does the association of the Spirit with the Father and the Son argue for the Spirit's personality, but the use of the word "name" in the singular also indicates that He is a person just as the others are. The apostolic benediction leads to the same conclusion: "The grace of the Lord Jesus Christ, and the love of God, and the communion of the Holy Ghost, be with you all. Amen" (II Cor. 13:14).

4. Further, the Holy Spirit is related to His own power and yet distinguished from it, so that one may not conclude that the Spirit is only power. "And Jesus returned in the power of the Spirit into Galilee" (Luke 4:14). A verse like this leads one to understand that the Spirit is a person who has power, and not that the Spirit is simply a powerful force or thing. Other examples of this distinction between the Spirit as a person and that person's power are found in Luke 1:35; Acts 10:38; Romans 15:13; I Corinthians 2:4. The phraseology of these verses would be useless and inexplicable repetition if the Holy Spirit were conceived as merely a power or influence and not a distinct personality with power of His own.

C. In Relation to Deity

The personality of the Holy Spirit argues for the deity of the Holy Spirit for two reasons:

1. A proper definition of personality supports the fact of the deity of the Spirit (as explained above).

2. The passages which prove personality name the other persons of the Trinity in such a close connection that they can be explained properly and fully only by understanding that the Holy Spirit is a divine person just as the Father and the Son are. These passages are the baptismal formula of Matthew 28:19 and the apostolic benediction of II Corinthians 13:14.

2

THE DEITY OF THE HOLY SPIRIT

I. PROOFS

A. Appellations

THE FACT that the Holy Spirit bears divine names is a proof of His deity. Sixteen times He is related by name to the other two persons of the Trinity. For example, He is called "the Spirit of our God" by Paul in I Corinthians 6:11. Again, in Greek texts of Acts 16:7 He is called "the Spirit of Jesus." In addition to these divine names, titles are given Him which reveal that the aspects of His ministry are the works of Deity. For instance, He is called "the Spirit of adoption" in Romans 8:15, which indicates that He plays a part in the adoption of the believer (cf. Gal. 4:1-5). The Lord Jesus Christ called the Holy Spirit "another Comforter" (John 14:16), a title which described a work which the Lord had been doing up to that time for the disciples. Such appellations of the Spirit reveal Him as equal in name, power, and performance with the Father and with the Son—a fact which is possible only if He too is divine.

B. Attributes

An attribute is a quality or characteristic inherent in a being. The attributes of God are those qualities or characteristics which belong to Him. The Bible, of course, ascribes many attributes to the Holy Spirit. If these are the attributes of Deity, then one can only conclude that the Spirit is divine. What attributes characterize the Holy Spirit?

1. *The Spirit is said to possess omniscience*—"For what man knoweth the things of a man, save the spirit of man which is in him? even so the things of God knoweth no man, but the Spirit of God. Now we have received, not the spirit of the world, but the spirit which is of God; that we might know the things that are freely given to us of God" (I Cor. 2:11-12).

2. *The Spirit is said to possess omnipresence*—"Whither shall

17

I go from thy spirit? or whither shall I flee from thy presence?"
(Ps. 139:7). The omnipresence of the Spirit and the omnipresence of God are equally comforting to the Psalmist.

3. *The Spirit is said to possess omnipotence,* by the act of creating—"The Spirit of God hath made me, and the breath of the
Almighty hath given me life" (Job 33:4), and by contrast with
man's limited power (Zech. 4:6). If the Spirit has omnipotence,
and if omnipotence is an attribute possessed only by God, then
the Spirit must be God.

4. *The Spirit is said to be truth*—"And it is the Spirit that
beareth witness, because the Spirit is truth" (I John 5:6*b*). The
Lord Jesus made the same claim in John 14:6, and if the Second
Person is divine, the Spirit is also.

5. *The Spirit is called the Holy Spirit* (Luke 11:13). While
man may possess a relative holiness, absolute holiness belongs
to God; and since this holiness is ascribed to the Spirit in His
very name, this is an indication of His deity.

6. *The Spirit is said to be a life-giver,* for He is called the
"Spirit of life" (Rom. 8:2; cf. v. 11). Only Deity can impart life.

7. *The Spirit is said to possess creative wisdom*—"Who hath directed the Spirit of the Lord, or being his counsellor hath taught
him?" (Isa. 40:13).

Thus the Holy Spirit is said to possess attributes which belong
to God, something possible only if He is Deity.

C. Actions

Many of the works of the Holy Spirit are those which can be
performed only by God Himself. Such actions would, therefore,
demonstrate the deity of the Spirit.

1. *The act of creation*—"And the earth was without form, and
void; and darkness was upon the face of the deep. And the Spirit
of God moved upon the face of the waters" (Gen. 1:2). As with
many other references to the "Spirit of God" in the Old Testament, one may rightly ask whether the reference is clearly to the
Third Person of the Trinity or merely to "potency in God." In
other words, does the Old Testament term refer to a principle or
a person? Leupold has given a balanced answer: "Absolutely none
other than the Holy Spirit is here under consideration. . . . It may
require the full light of New Testament revelation to enable us
to discern that the Spirit of God here is the same as He who in

the New Testament is seen to be the Holy Spirit; but having that light, we need not hesitate to believe that it sheds clear light back on the Old Testament usage of the expression. . . . Does it not seem reasonable that the Spirit of inspiration should have so worded the words that bear upon His activity that, when the full New Testament revelation has come, all statements concerning the Spirit are in perfect harmony with this later revelation?"[1] This, then, may be understood as a reference to the Holy Spirit's part in the work of creation.

A few of the other passages which link the Spirit to the formative cause of all life are Job 26:13; 27:3; Psalm 33:6; 104:30. The creation of the universe is not the work of man. It was the work of God and of the Holy Spirit; therefore, the Spirit is God.

2. *The act of inspiration*—"For the prophecy came not in old time by the will of man: but holy men of God spake as they were moved by the Holy Ghost" (II Peter 1:21). The inspiration of Scripture is described in another passage by the term "God-breathed" (II Tim. 3:16). What is meant by inspiration need not detain us at this juncture. The point is that the Scriptures are from God, according to II Timothy 3:16, and that they are from the Holy Spirit, according to II Peter 1:21. This work of inspiration of Scripture is never ascribed to man and therefore demonstrates the deity of the Spirit to whom it is ascribed.

3. *The act of begetting Christ*—"And the angel answered and said unto her, The Holy Ghost shall come upon thee, and the power of the Highest shall overshadow thee: therefore also that holy thing which shall be born of thee shall be called the Son of God" (Luke 1:35). In this single verse the power of the Spirit and the power of God ("the Highest") are equal causes of the virgin birth of Christ. This, too, demonstrates the deity of the Spirit.

These three works are distinctively works of God which man cannot perform and which, therefore, indicate the deity of the Holy Spirit. There are other activities of the Spirit, and man can perform works similar to them though not in the same manner or with the same results. While man can convince, generate, comfort and intercede, these works of the Spirit are further proofs of His deity because in the last analysis God alone can perform them absolutely.

[1]H. C. Leupold, *Exposition of Genesis* (Columbus: Wartburg Press, 1942), pp. 49-50.

4. *The work of convincing*—"And when he is come, he will reprove the world of sin, and of righteousness, and of judgment" (John 16:8).

5. *The work of regenerating*—"That which is born of the flesh is flesh; and that which is born of the Spirit is spirit" (John 3:6).

6. *The work of comforting*—"And I will pray the Father, and he shall give you another Comforter, that he may abide with you forever" (John 14:16). The everlasting presence of the Comforter is not a human work.

7. *The work of interceding*—"Likewise the Spirit also helpeth our infirmities: for we know not what we should pray for as we ought: but the Spirit itself maketh intercession for us with groanings which cannot be uttered" (Rom. 8:26).

8. *The work of sanctifying* (or setting apart)—"But we are bound to give thanks always to God for you, brethren beloved of the Lord, because God hath from the beginning chosen you to salvation through sanctification of the Spirit and belief of the truth" (II Thess. 2:13).

D. Associations

1. *With Jehovah.* One of the strongest proofs of the deity of the Holy Spirit is the scriptural identification of the Spirit with Jehovah of the Old Testament (cf. Acts 28:25 and Isa. 6:1-13; cf. Heb. 10:15-17 and Jer. 31:31-34).

2. *With God.* Blasphemy of and lying to the Holy Spirit are the same as doing these things to God (Matt. 12:31-32; Acts 5:3-4).

3. *With the Father and the Son.* Full association on equal terms further indicates the deity of the Spirit (Matt. 28:19; II Cor. 13:14).

II. PROCESSION

A. Its Meaning

How the persons of the Trinity are related to each other is difficult to express. The relation of the Spirit to the other persons of the Trinity is usually expressed by the term "procession." Therefore, the procession of the Holy Spirit means that in His being and eternity He is related to the Father and to the Son in that He proceeded from them. Another definition states that procession (or spiration as it is sometimes called) is "that eternal and necessary act of the First and Second Persons of the Trinity whereby they, within the divine Being, become the ground of the personal subsistence of the Holy Spirit, and put the Third Person in possession of the whole divine essence, without any division, alienation or change."[2] The concept was formulated in the Constantinopolitan Creed (381) with the addition of the filioque ("and Son") clause at the Synod of Toledo (589). Throughout history the Western church has affirmed the procession from the Father *and Son,* whereas the Eastern church has not.

B. Its Proof

The major proof text is John 15:26. The present tense in the verse ("proceedeth") is understood to refer to the eternality of the Spirit's procession. That He proceeds from the Son as well is supported by such texts as Galatians 4:6; Romans 8:9; John 16:7.

C. Its Distinction from Generation

The eternal relationship of the Son to the Father is termed generation. It is the work of the Father only, while procession of the Spirit involves both Father and Son. Logically (but in no way chronologically), generation of the Son precedes procession of the Spirit. It is fully recognized that both terms are inadequate, but no one has been able to improve on them. What single words could ever express the eternal relationships of the Trinity? Certainly the terms imply no inferiority of one person to any of the others. Neither do the words *First* and *Second* and *Third* when used of the persons of the Godhead imply any chronological order. Generation and procession are attempts to denote *eternal* relationships involving distinctions between equal persons.

III. PROBLEMS

A. Is There a Difference Between the Spirit of God and the Spirit of Jesus?

Some versions of Acts 16:7 read "Spirit of Jesus," but this is a reference to the same Holy Spirit of God. In Romans 8:9 the title "Spirit of Christ" is likewise simply another designation for the Holy Spirit. There is only one Spirit (Eph. 4:4; I Cor. 12:11,

[2]Louis Berkhof, *Systematic Theology* (Grand Rapids: Wm. B. Eerdmans Publishing Co., 1946), p. 97.

13) . These references no more refer to different spirits than the grace of God (Gal. 2:21) and the grace of Christ (Gal. 1:6) refer to two different graces.

B. What Is the Meaning of Seven Spirits?

At least four times in the Revelation (1:4; 3:1; 4:5; 5:6) reference is made to seven spirits. Since there is only one Spirit, these must be pleonasms or full ways of expression just as Revelation 5:6 is in speaking of the Lamb with seven horns and seven eyes.

3

REPRESENTATIONS OF THE HOLY SPIRIT

I. DESIRABILITY

THE NEW TESTAMENT gives complete sanction to the field of typology and illustration. Events (Heb. 4:11), institutions (Heb. 8:5), and persons (James 5:10) are so sanctioned. But for several reasons the whole field of typology and illustration has come into disrepute. One reason is lack of clear definition. A type, for instance, needs to be clearly defined, precisely conceived (this means no stretch of the imagination allowed), and distinctly segregated from illustration. The loose and indiscriminate use of the word *type* has been detrimental to the truth.

Another reason for this disrepute has been the abuse of typology. Imagination is stretched, discernment thrown to the wind, and an "anything goes" approach has been taken. But the activity of typological quacks ought all the more to make the careful Bible student want to become an expert in the subject.

A third reason for avoiding the subject is lack of perception. There is no doubt that the study of types requires a kind of spiritual capacity and habitual exercise of discerning insight into the truth of the Scriptures that all do not possess. Since types, illustrations, and symbols are pictures, there is required, in order to understand them, thorough knowledge of the realities which they picture.

II. DEFINITIONS

A. Type

A type is a divinely purposed illustration which prefigures its corresponding reality. This definition has three important elements.

1. A type must be *divinely purposed*. This distinguishes it from events or circumstances which are normal or, so to speak, accidental. For instance, certain events in the life of Joseph were

apparently divinely purposed, while many others were perfectly normal to his life and thus not typical. Joseph is nowhere specifically called a type of Christ, but it is difficult not to see in his experiences with his brethren that which prefigured the experiences of Christ in His life. The conspiracy of Joseph's brethren to kill him, his taking a Gentile bride, his subsequent reconciliation with his brethren and their exaltation were certainly not ordinary events, but were divinely purposed (cf. Gen. 37:18 and Matt. 26:3-4; cf. Gen. 41:1-45 and Acts 15:14; cf. Gen. 45:1-15 and Rom. 11:26).

2. The word *illustration* is used in the definition as a reminder that there need not be an exact one-to-one correspondence between a type and its corresponding reality or antitype. In other words, some latitude is allowable between the type and its antitype. For instance, there have to be normal historical and geographical elements in an event which may be a type, to provide the necessary background for the particular divinely purposed part of that event which is the type. Types are given in normal historical situations, but all the aspects of those situations are not necessarily typical.

3. The verb *prefigure* indicates that included in a type-antitype relation there must be a separate and distinct entity which is the type and a separate and distinct entity which is the antitype. Oil, therefore, is a type of the Holy Spirit, for the use of oil in the Old Testament as a distinct substance prefigured in several divinely purposed ways the subsequent work of the Spirit.

B. Illustration

To illustrate is to make clear by elucidation or adornment or pictures. In an illustration it is not necessary to have the concept of prefiguring as in a type. In other words, an illustration is suggested by the reality (or antitype) itself. Obviously the word *illustration* is a much broader one than type, for it is not so restricted. The servant story of Genesis 24 is an excellent illustration of the Holy Spirit.

It seems best to use the word *type* rather carefully and guardedly. If something is not clearly a type, then call it an illustration. Other words, like *emblem* and *symbol,* may also be legitimate labels for certain of the biblical representations of the Holy Spirit, but the distinction between these concepts is not always clear-cut. Therefore it is best to use the broad category of illustration to include all those representations which are not specifically types.

III. DESCRIPTIONS

All the biblical descriptions of the person and work of the Holy Spirit, whether in type, by emblem, with symbol, or by illustration, help better to understand Him. Therefore, each one has its important contribution to the doctrine. They are listed here alphabetically, rather than by categories.

A. Breath (see *wind* below)

B. Clothing (Luke 24:49, ASV)

Christ was evidently predicting the coming of the Spirit at Pentecost when He filled the disciples. This emblem has four features.

1. *Power* (because it is clothing which God puts on us, not that with which we clothe ourselves).

2. *Protection.* Just as clothing is a covering, so the Holy Spirit protects those whom He covers.

3. *Holiness* (again because it is from God, cf. Eph. 4:24).

4. Pictorial emblem of our relationship as *belonging* to God and representing Him (cf. Luke 15:22; e.g., the commencement gown and hood represent the university from which the wearer received the honor of which the regalia is an emblem).

C. Dove (Matt. 3:16; Mark 1:10; Luke 3:22; John 1:32)

All four Gospels mention that at Christ's baptism the Holy Spirit descended on Him like a dove. The emblem speaks of:

1. The purity of the Spirit (cf. Matt. 10:16, where "harmless" ought to be rendered "unmixed" or "pure").

2. The heavenly origin of the Spirit (the dove descended from the opened heavens).

3. Peace (the dove rested on Christ).

Except for the mention of the dove released from the ark after the Flood, all Old Testament references to doves are in connection with the sacrifices, which were typical of Christ and unrelated to the doctrine of the Holy Spirit.

D. Earnest (II Cor. 1:22; 5:5; Eph. 1:14)

The Feast of Firstfruits as an earnest of the harvest was well known. The principal idea in the earnest is *pledge*. The presence of the Holy Spirit in the believer's heart is the pledged guarantee on the part of God that he will receive all the promised future blessings of his salvation. The fact that God gives the earnest of the Spirit binds Him to complete fully the salvation which He has begun in the heart. Even in human affairs, once earnest money has been given, the purchaser is pledged to go through with a transaction. What a sure guarantee is the presence of the Spirit, God's earnest, that He will never fail any of His promises connected with our salvation!

E. Fire (Acts 2:3)

It was not actually fire that appeared on the day of Pentecost but cloven tongues. Because they were cloven they appeared as fire, which shoots forth in tongues or fingers of flame; but it was tongues that sat on each of the disciples, not fire. However, this manifestation which is described like fire and which appeared when they were filled with the Holy Spirit would have had significant meaning to the people so familiar with the Old Testament use of fire as an emblem. It conveyed:

1. The presence of the Lord (cf. Exodus 3:2).
2. The approval of the Lord (cf. Lev. 9:24).
3. The protection of the Lord (Exodus 13:21).
4. The judging, sanctifying, cleansing power of the Lord (Lev. 10:2; Isa. 6:1-8).

What is the meaning of the announcement of John the Baptist that Christ would baptize "with the Holy Ghost and with fire" (Matt. 3:11)? One interpretation says that this was completely fulfilled at Pentecost. Another suggests that the baptism with the Spirit was fulfilled on the day of Pentecost but the fire is a general reference to the entire work of sanctification of the Spirit throughout the age. A third interpretation says that John as the last of the Old Testament prophets was speaking of Pentecost in his reference to the baptism with the Spirit, and of the judgment at the second coming of Christ in the reference to fire. That there is a reference to the second advent seems to be consistent with the context (cf. Matt. 3:12).

F. Oil (Luke 4:18; Acts 10:38; II Cor. 1:21; I John 2:20)

Oil is a type of the Holy Spirit because of its divinely purposed use in the Old Testament. In relation to the ministry of the Holy Spirit it prefigures three things.

1. The necessity of the work of the Spirit in preparation for ministry was typified in the Old Testament by the anointing with oil at the induction of priests (Exodus 40:9-16; Lev. 8; Isa. 61:1-2, cf. Luke 4:18). The ministry of the Spirit is indispensable for a fruitful ministry for the believer today (Acts 1:8).

2. The sole light in the tabernacle was provided by the holy oil in the lampstand which lighted the place where God was worshiped, the place which in every particular foreshadowed the work of Christ (Exodus 27:20-21). Likewise, today, it is the Holy Spirit who throws the spotlight upon Him who is the truth and who glorifies Christ before the eyes of the Christian (John 16:13-15; I John 2:20).

3. Oil was also used in the cleansing and sanctifying of priests and lepers (Lev. 8:30; 14:17). Similarly the Spirit sanctifies believers in this day.

G. Seal (II Cor. 1:22; Eph. 1:13; 4:30)

When a person believes in Christ he is sealed immediately and permanently with the Holy Spirit. Technically, the Holy Spirit is the seal rather than the one who does the sealing. The seal as the token of the completion of a transaction was known in the Old Testament (Jer. 32:9-10). The Holy Spirit seal on the believer indicates:

1. Ownership by God.

2. Security that is permanently guaranteed (for only God can break the seal, and He has promised not to do so).

3. Authority over what He owns.

4. The realization of all promised blessings at the day of redemption (Eph. 4:30).

H. Servant (Gen. 24)

The story of Abraham's servant seeking a wife for Isaac illustrates in many points the ministry of the Holy Spirit.

1. Just as the purpose of the servant was to serve and to speak

only of his master, so the Holy Spirit does not speak from Himself but reveals Christ (John 16:13).

2. The mission of the servant was to seek a bride for Isaac. Today the Holy Spirit adds to the Body of Christ those who believe and who altogether form His Bride.

3. The servant gave gifts to the bride just as spiritual gifts are given today through the Holy Spirit (I Cor. 12:11).

I. Water (John 4:14; 7:38-39)

The Lord Jesus compared the future ministry of the Spirit to water springing up and flowing out of the believer's life. Therefore this emblem signifies:

1. The eternal life which springs up from that which was entirely barren before.

2. The abundance of the "life more abundant" which Christ gives.

3. Service, for out of the believer shall flow rivers of living water to others.

J. Wind (John 3:8; Acts 2:1-2 [?])

The Lord illustrated the work of the Holy Spirit in regeneration by using wind. This indicates the work of the Holy Spirit in the new creation as having several characteristics.

1. His work is invisible. No one can see the wind, though one can see the results and effects of the wind. Likewise, the new birth is in itself invisible, although the results of it in a changed life are quite visible.

2. The Spirit's work is sovereign; that is, He touches whom He will, just as the wind blows where it pleases (John 3:8). No man can claim the right to expect the Spirit to regenerate him. He works according to the sovereign purposes of God in elective grace.

3. The work of the Spirit in the new birth is heavenly. The Lord sharply contrasted the earthly birth with the new, heavenly birth. The latter is "from above." The wind, too, is from the heavens and blows upon the earth.

4. Wind is powerful, as anyone who has seen a tornado or hurricane well knows. The Spirit's work in the new creation is also powerful, though not to destruction as wind often is, but to regeneration.

On the day of Pentecost the coming of the Spirit was accompanied by a sound *as of* the rushing of a mighty wind. Acts 2:2 does not say that the disciples felt wind, but that they heard a windlike sound.

No one who studies the doctrine of the Holy Spirit should ever neglect these types and illustrations of the Spirit. They can often help in elaborating and accentuating the explicit teaching of Scripture on the Holy Spirit. They will help to clarify the truth to the student's own heart, and they certainly provide excellent preaching material for presenting the truth to others.

4

THE HOLY SPIRIT IN RELATION
TO CREATION

THE WORK OF CREATION is generally ascribed to God without distinguishing the persons within the Godhead as far as the particular work of each is concerned. In speaking of the work of creation the Scriptures usually attribute it to God, although in the New Testament creation is ascribed to Christ. However, the Holy Spirit, too, had His part, and the Bible testifies to this clearly.

I. THE PROOF OF THE SPIRIT'S PART IN CREATION

A. Proof from the Scriptures

1. Genesis 1:2. The work of the Spirit in creation is not expressly mentioned until after the original creation (assuming that v. 1 records the fact of the original creation and v. 2 begins the account of a restoration). Of course as a member of the Trinity He participated in the act of original creation in 1:1. Whatever this involved, it apparently included some sort of life-giving or life-sustaining function with regard to the earth at that time.

2. Psalm 33:6. The word "breath" is, of course, the word "spirit." Whether this is a reference to the Holy Spirit, however, is really not conclusive, for the "spirit of his mouth" cannot be said to refer clearly to a person, to say nothing of clearly referring to the Third Person of the Trinity. Some, nevertheless, do understand it as a reference to the Holy Spirit.

3. Psalm 104:30. This seems to be a clearer reference to the Holy Spirit, although it cannot be positively related to the creative work recorded in Genesis 1—2. The reference to sea animals in verse 26 and the use of bara' in verse 30 may indicate the Genesis creation.

4. Isaiah 40:12-14. In these verses the Spirit is directly connected with the planning and management of the universe.

5. Job 26:13. Although some translations (e.g., RSV) translate "Spirit" by "breath," there seems no good reason for not translating it "Spirit" and recognizing it as a reference to the Holy Spirit's part in creation. The only possible weakening of the force of the verse would be in the fact that this may be merely Job's opinion and not the statement of express divine revelation. Inspiration, of course, only guarantees the accuracy of the record.

6. Job 33:4. This verse refers to the Spirit's work in creating man.

The Holy Spirit's distinct part in creation is sufficiently supported by these verses.

B. Proof from the Use of *Elohim*

Although the form *Elohim* is a genuine plural, it is undoubtedly a plural of majesty rather than a numerical plural; that is, it speaks of God's greatness, not of the Trinity. It signifies God as the fullness of Deity. When referring to the true God, it is generally used with other parts of speech in the singular. Nevertheless, the word does leave room for the later New Testament revelation of the Trinity, and while the Old Testament revelation did not teach the doctrine of the Trinity, it allowed for it. Therefore, in the light of New Testament truth concerning the Trinity, the many references in Genesis 1 which refer to *Elohim* as the creator incorporate the work of the Son and of the Spirit along with that of the Father. Thus *Elohim* in the light of New Testament revelation is a further proof of the fact that the Holy Spirit shared the work of creation.

II. THE PARTICULARS OF THE SPIRIT'S PART IN CREATION

A. Life

This is the basic work of the Spirit in many areas, including that of creation (cf. John 6:63; II Cor. 3:6). He gives life to the creation (Ps. 104:30; Job 33:4).

B. Order

The creation is one of order. This is seen in the waters, the heavens, and the earth (Isa. 40:12), and particularly in the orderly processes in the heavens (Job 26:13).

separable. And the Bible claims such for itself (Matt. 5:17; Gal. 3:16).

2. The Bible then would have authority, for infallibility brings with it absolute authority.

3. Such an inspired record could only have been given in words and not merely thoughts, for there is not any genuine or accurate thought communication without its being conveyed in words. Thoughts without words are unexpressed, and accurate expression of thoughts can be accomplished only in accurate words.

The entirety of God's revelation is, of course, not contained in the Bible. He was revealed through the oral messages of the prophets; He has also revealed Himself to some extent in nature; and He has been fully revealed in Christ. But revelation always concerns the material which God has used to reveal Himself, while inspiration concerns the method by which the material written in the Bible was recorded. For further comparison, illumination concerns the understanding of the meaning of God's revelation, whether oral or written.

II. THE AUTHOR AND MEANS OF REVELATION

The principal human instrument of revelation in the Old Testament was the prophet. Although the giving of revelation was not limited to the prophet (e.g., it also came through people like Eve, Cain, Hagar), no one could qualify as a true prophet unless he had received revelation. In New Testament times the apostles and those closely associated with them were the chief human agents of revelation.

However, behind the human instruments was the author of revelation, the Holy Spirit. Peter, referring to Old Testament prophecy, declared that "men spake from God, being moved by the Holy Spirit" (II Peter 1:21, ASV). The agents were men; the source was God; and the single author moving the human instruments was the Holy Spirit.

This inclusive statement of Peter is supported by many examples elsewhere in Scripture. Old Testament prophets declare that they spoke by means of the Spirit (II Sam. 23:2; Ezek. 2:2; Micah 3:8). Furthermore, the New Testament attributes many Old Testament Scriptures to the Spirit (Matt. 22:43; Acts 1:16; 4:25). On the basis of such references, it is quite safe to conclude that the Holy Spirit had a large place in the giving of God's revelation.

The means of revelation were varied.

1. Revelation came through the spoken word. On many occasions this word was spoken vocally and directly from God (Exodus 19:9; I Sam. 3:1-14), though in other instances it was given to the heart and mind of the prophet, who then spoke it to the people. The direct voice of God speaking on these occasions is a vivid reminder that revelation is specific, clear, and in words. That the Holy Spirit is the particular person of the Trinity who functioned in the giving of God's revelation in words is evident from such passages as Acts 28:25 in comparison with Isaiah 6: 9-10.

2. Revelation came through dreams. This means was used many times in early days (Gen. 20, 31, 37, 40—41) and will be used again in the future (Joel 2:28-29). Generally dreams were not the method used in giving revelation to prophets, but they were often used in relation to heathen men.

3. Revelation came through visions. In a vision the human agent was a more active participant than in a dream. The state of sleep did not seem to be as necessary in the receiving of a vision as it was in a dream (Gen. 15:1; 46:2; Isa. 1:1; 6:1; Ezek. 1: 3). And yet the recipient was not merely awake as at other times, but his soul and senses seemed to be elevated to some higher state.

4. Revelation came through the ministry of the Spirit to New Testament writers. Before the Lord Jesus left the earth He promised that the Spirit would minister to the disciples in recalling to their minds the things which He had taught them (John 14:26).

5. Revelation came through the person and ministry of Christ. This avenue of revelation was not connected with the work of the Spirit except as He was involved in the life of Christ.

III. THE AUTHOR OF INSPIRATION

Although the Scriptures were breathed out from God (II Tim. 3:16), the particular person of the Godhead who bore along the human authors was the Holy Spirit. The result of this divine-human effort was the inspired text of the Bible. That the Spirit is the particular agent involved in this work of inspiration is demonstrated in the following ways:

1. The Old Testament witnesses to the fact that the Spirit spoke through its writers (II Sam. 23:2-3) . This specific reference to the Spirit is reinforced by the many references to the fact that the Lord spoke through men. "Thus saith the Lord" resounds everywhere in the pages of the Old Testament.

2. The New Testament assigns Old Testament quotations to the Holy Spirit as their author. Christ, in His encounter with the Pharisees, quoted from Psalm 110 written by David and attributed to the Holy Spirit divine authorship of that psalm of David. Christ declared: "David himself said in the Holy Spirit, The Lord said unto my Lord, Sit thou on my right hand, till I make thine enemies the footstool of thy feet" (Mark 12:36, ASV) . In connection with the replacement for Judas, Peter, quoting from Psalm 41 attributed it to the work of the Spirit (Acts 1:16) . The same was done with Psalm 2 when Peter led the group in the prayer recorded in Acts 4:24-25. Paul, also, quoted from the Old Testament and assigned its authorship to the Holy Spirit (Acts 28:25; cf. Isa. 6:9-10) . The writer to the Hebrews did the same in at least two places in his epistle (3:7; 10:15-16) .

3. The promise of Christ indicated that it would be the work of the Spirit to provide accurate recounting of the events of His life (John 14:26) .

IV. THE SCOPE OF OLD TESTAMENT MATERIAL INCLUDED IN INSPIRATION

Plenary inspiration means, of course, that the entire record is inspired. However, there were different kinds of material included in the record.

1. Records of the unknown past. In guaranteeing the truthfulness and accuracy of the records of the unknown past, inspiration guided the writing of that which was made known by revelation to the authors. Even if documents were used in the compiling of the final books, inspiration was still operative in superintending what was used from existing documents. However, the revealing of these matters concerning the unknown past was probably largely accomplished through direct revelation.

2. Records of history. Much of the Old Testament and of the Gospels falls into this category. Inspiration again guarantees the accuracy of what is recorded, and guided the choice of material

as well. Too, if documents were used, this did not obviate the need for the work of the Holy Spirit (cf. Luke 1:1-4).

3. Records of dictated material. The Ten Commandments, for instance, were dictated by God and merely transcribed by Moses. In dictated portions, of course, the writers' distinctive traits are least noticed. It should be carefully noted that only a relatively small proportion of the Bible falls into this category of dictated material. The doctrine of verbal, plenary inspiration is not the dictation theory.

4. Records of prophetic messages. This included both the contemporary prophetic utterance and the forecasting of future events. In relation to the latter, the prophet did not always understand what he wrote, but its accuracy was nevertheless guarded by the operation of the Spirit in inspiration (cf. I Peter 1:10-11; II Peter 1:21). The accuracy of many of the prophecies concerning the future—particularly Old Testament ones—can easily be confirmed by their subsequent fulfillment.

5. Records of devotional literature. Some of the devotional literature included in the Bible poses a problem in relation to the doctrine of inspiration. Does inspiration guarantee only the accurate record of these thoughts, or are they to be understood as a true revelation of the mind and will of God? How can one be sure that the human experience being recorded is a valid one? Inspiration, of course, does assure of the accuracy of the records, and in most instances it is apparent that it also guided the authors so that those experiences which would give us a true picture of God and of valid experiences with God were the ones which were recorded.

V. THE INSPIRATION OF THE NEW TESTAMENT

The proof of the inspiration of the New Testament must be approached in a slightly different manner from that of the Old. A verse like II Timothy 3:16 certainly includes all the Old Testament but not all, if any, of the New. Nevertheless, the inspiration of the New Testament is affirmed in the following ways:

1. It is authenticated by Christ. The Lord placed the oral prophetic ministry of those who proclaimed the message in His name on a plane of equal authority with Himself. The message of both the seventy and the twelve (at their first commissioning)

was so authenticated (Luke 10:16; Matt. 10:14). Too, the disciples were assured of this authority in the upper room just before His death (John 13:20). Furthermore, on the same occasion, they were promised the aid of the Holy Spirit in bringing to their remembrance after His death the things which Christ had taught them (John 14:26). This great promise is an incontrovertible preauthentication of what was later recorded by these disciples in the books of the New Testament. This promise was broadened to include not only those things which Christ had personally taught them while on earth but also those things which He would subsequently reveal to them after His resurrection and the descent of the Spirit on the day of Pentecost (John 16:14). These two verses together (John 14:26 and 16:14) incorporate all the subsequently written record of the New Testament in and under His authentication and authority.

2. It is asserted by the writers of the New Testament. The writers of the New Testament were conscious of the authority of their writings. They seemed to realize that they were adding to the body of Scriptures and that the content of their writings had equal authority.

For instance, after Paul wrote correcting some of the difficulties in the Corinthian church he declared: "If any man think himself to be a prophet, or spiritual, let him acknowledge that the things that I write unto you are the commandments of the Lord" (I Cor. 14:37). In correcting laziness among the Thessalonians he concluded: "And if any man obey not our word by this epistle, note that man, and have no company with him, that he may be ashamed" (II Thess. 3:14). (See also Gal. 1:7-8 and I Thess. 4: 2, 15.)

3. It is attested to by the apostles of each other's writings. Not only were the writers of the New Testament conscious of the operation of the Spirit's work of inspiration in the case of their own writings, but they also attested to it in the case of each other's writings. Paul, in proving a point about elders, quoted from Deuteronomy 25:4 and Luke 10:7 in I Timothy 5:18. He called both quotations "Scripture." Peter bore his testimony to the inspired character of Paul's writings, calling all of them "Scripture" (II Peter 3:16). This he did in spite of the fact that he had to confess his own inability to understand fully these inspired writings of Paul.

4. It is assumed by the Holy Spirit by His manner of quoting the Old Testament. What is usually considered a problem is in reality a proof of the inspiration of the New Testament. For one thing, the formulas by which the New Testament writers introduce their quotations commonly refer to God as the author. This is the case even when the quotation is not a saying of God so recorded in the Old Testament but the word of Scripture (cf. Matt. 19:4-5; Acts 4:25; 13:35; Heb. 1:5-8; 3:7; 4:4). Such could be the case only if the writer was treating all Scripture as a declaration of God.

For another thing, Old Testament quotations are sometimes personified so that the actions of God are ascribed to the Scripture (cf. Rom. 9:17; Gal. 3:8). This could only be done if the writer in his own mind was habitually identifying the text of Scripture with God speaking. Furthermore, the use of the term *law* or *prophets* in references which belong to parts of the Hebrew canon other than the law or the prophets shows that the whole Old Testament was considered equally binding and authoritative.

Finally, it can be demonstrated that the New Testament writers quoted the Old Testament in a manner consistent only with the highest regard for the texts quoted. This involved their translating the quotations from the Hebrew text into Greek, and no translation is as exact as the original. When they used the Greek Septuagint they often did it because the point they were making was clearer in the Septuagint. The discovery of the Dead Sea Scrolls opens the possibility that occasionally the Septuagint may have represented a better primitive Hebrew original. In such instances, then, it would have been more accurate to quote from the Septuagint than from the Masoretic text.

The fact that Old Testament passages were often paraphrased is no problem. The minds of the writers were full of Scripture and they did not have quotation marks to employ in their writing. Verbal inspiration assures in such cases that the words of their paraphrases were also exactly what God wanted to use in conveying His message. Sometimes paraphrases or summaries were preferable to long quotations. But in all these methods it is the Holy Spirit, the ultimate author, using human instruments by superintending their writing so that God's complete message was recorded. And the fact that the Spirit did use free quotations or even quotations from a translation (LXX) could only be done if He is the author of both Testaments.

5. It was accepted by the early church. The fact that the canon of the New Testament was accepted by the church because the apostolic authority of the individual books was recognized is further attestation to the inspiration of those books. While this acceptance was not universally agreed upon immediately, it was agreed on by A.D. 397 and universally so. Indeed, the question of New Testament canonicity has not been a problem in the church since then.

To be sure, these general principles do not deal with specific examples and may not solve every problem (though they probably will provide *a* solution to every problem cited). The believer need not give up his investigative mind in order to hold verbal, plenary inspiration. But in his investigations the words of Warfield are worth keeping in mind: "Every unharmonized passage remains a case of difficult harmony and does not pass into the category of objections to plenary inspiration. It can pass into the category of objections only if we are prepared to affirm that we clearly see that it is, on any conceivable hypothesis of its meaning, clearly inconsistent with the Biblical doctrine of inspiration. In that case we would no doubt need to give up the Biblical doctrine of inspiration; but with it we must also give up our confidence in the Biblical writers as teachers of doctrine."[1]

[1]B. B. Warfield, *The Inspiration and Authority of the Bible* (Nutley, N.J.: Presbyterian and Reformed Publishing Co., 1948), p. 220.

6

THE HOLY SPIRIT IN RELATION TO MAN IN THE OLD TESTAMENT

THE WORK OF THE SPIRIT in relation to man in the Old Testament was not exactly similar to that which He does today for man. Pentecost marked the beginning of certain distinctive differences, although no one should get the impression that His ministry was rare or sparse in Old Testament times. When we speak of the Spirit "coming" at Pentecost we do not mean that He was absent from the earth before then. He took up His residence in believers at Pentecost although He was present always before.

I. THE NATURE OF HIS WORK

A. Selective Indwelling

By the word *selective* it is indicated that the indwelling of the Spirit in Old Testament times was not necessarily universally experienced among God's people. His relationship to people is comprehended by three words.

First, it is said that the Spirit was *in* certain ones. Pharaoh recognized the indwelling of the Spirit in Joseph (Gen. 41:38). Whether Pharaoh understood this as a reference to the Holy Spirit may well be questioned, but that it was the ministry of the Spirit in Joseph seems clear from later revelation. The Spirit was clearly said to be in Joshua, and this is the reason for God's choosing him (Num. 27:18). Further, the Spirit was said to be in Daniel (Dan. 4:8; 5:11-14; 6:3). The preposition *in* in all these verses is *beth* in Hebrew.

Second, the Spirit is said to have come *upon* many. The preposition used to describe this relationship of the Spirit is *al*, and this relationship was experienced by many people in Old Testament times (Judges 3:10; 6:34; 11:29; 13:25; I Sam. 10:9-10; 16: 13). Is there any difference between the Spirit's being in and the Spirit's coming upon men? We are probably not to understand any significant difference except that the idea of coming

41

upon seems to imply the temporary and transitory character of the Spirit's relationship to Old Testament saints.

Third, the Spirit is said to have *filled* some. This is recorded of Bezaleel in relation to his leadership of the craftsmen working on the tabernacle (Exodus 31:3; 35:31). One may assume that this special filling for service presupposed the Spirit's indwelling or at least His having come upon him.

What do these examples indicate? Simply that, although the Spirit did indwell men in Old Testament times, it was a selective ministry, both in regard to whom He indwelt and for how long. Can this relationship be summarized in any simple way? Yes, for the Lord summarized it by telling His disciples that up to that time the Spirit had been abiding with them, though on and after the day of Pentecost He would be in them (John 14:17). From this statement two things are clear concerning the Old Testament work of the Spirit:

1. It was not erratic, even though it may have been limited as to persons included and the length of time they experienced His ministry. The word "abideth," in any case, does not indicate an erratic ministry.

2. Nevertheless, His ministry was different from that which began on Pentecost, for the Lord carefully characterized the ministry as "with" in contrast to "in," which began at Pentecost. Although in the Old Testament there were clear instances when the Spirit indwelt men, His ministry could not be described generally as a ministry of being in men but only with them. Many things may not be clear in this contrast between "with" and "in," but a contrast is clear.

B. Restraint of Sin

One of the clear ministries of the Spirit in the Old Testament was that of restraining sin. This He did from the dawn of human history (Gen. 6:3). His very names and titles, too, must have had a restraining effect on men as they considered Him (Neh. 9:20; Ps. 51:11).

C. Enablement for Service

Mention has already been made of Bezaleel's special enduement for service in the construction of the tabernacle (Exodus 31:3). This supernatural ability was not to the exclusion of his native ability but in addition to it. Some of the judges were given Spirit enablement (Judges 3:10; 6:34; 11:29). Samson's strength was produced by the Spirit's coming on him (Judges 14:6). When David was anointed king by Samuel "the Spirit of Jehovah came mightily upon David from that day forward" (I Sam. 16:13, ASV). The New Testament reveals that the Spirit in the prophets gave them discernment and wisdom (I Peter 1: 11).

II. THE LIMITATIONS OF HIS WORK

A. It Was Limited in Its Extent

References already cited clearly show that not all people enjoyed the enabling ministry of the Spirit. Even in Israel His enablement was not given universally, and those outside the commonwealth of Israel knew little if anything of His work on behalf of the individual. The fact that the new covenant promised for Israel a ministry of the Spirit in a greater way than they knew under the old covenant is further proof that His ministry under the old was limited (Isa. 59:21; Ezek. 39:29).

B. It Was Limited in Its Duration

In Old Testament times the Holy Spirit could be withdrawn from men. Samson was enabled by the Spirit from the time of Judges 13:25 until God withdrew the Spirit as recorded in Judges 16:20. Saul was laid hold of by the Spirit (I Sam. 10:10), though afterward the Spirit withdrew (I Sam. 16:14). After his great sin David pleaded with God not to withdraw His Spirit from him (Ps. 51:11) —a prayer which is never found in the New Testament.

In contrast to this temporary nature of the Spirit's relation to men in the Old Testament, the Lord promised that in this age the Spirit would be given them eternally: "And I will pray the Father, and he shall give you another Comforter, that he may be with you forever" (John 14:16, ASV). The universal (among believers) and permanent indwelling of the Spirit is distinctive to this age and was not experienced in Old Testament times.

C. It Was Limited in Its Effect

Although there was no ministry of the Spirit guaranteed universally to all individual Israelites, all Israel benefited from the

Spirit's ministry. It was a general ministry to the nation which other peoples did not enjoy, but indwelling of all individuals within that one nation was not a part of that ministry. Such verses as Nehemiah 9:20 and Isaiah 63:10-11, 14 indicate such a general ministry to the nation. But at the same time the effect of this ministry was not to baptize them into the Body of Christ as He does today. The very fact that the Lord indicated the baptism by the Spirit was future (Acts 1:5) shows that Old Testament saints did not experience it. Further, the power of a Spirit-overflowing life was also declared by Jesus to be future at the time of His ministry (John 7:37-39), thus indicating that this too was unknown, at least universally, in Old Testament times.

To sum up: The Holy Spirit did have a ministry to man in Old Testament times. Indeed, it was a bountiful ministry in many cases. However, it was limited to certain Israelites (except for the general ministry of restraining evil, which affected all men); and although He did dwell in, come upon, and sometimes fill men, He did not do these things universally or permanently, even in Israel. Too, He did not perform certain other ministries until the day of Pentecost.

7

THE HOLY SPIRIT IN RELATION
TO JESUS CHRIST

I. THE BIRTH OF CHRIST

A. The Agent of the Virgin Birth

IT WAS ANNOUNCED to Mary by the angel Gabriel that the baby to be born to her would be conceived by the Holy Spirit (Luke 1:35). The same fact was made known to Joseph (Matt. 1:20). Elsewhere we are told that the Father prepared Christ a body (Heb. 10:5) and that the Son took upon Himself flesh and blood (as if it were an act of His own will, Heb. 2:14). It is correct to say then that Christ was begotten of the Holy Spirit, although God is the one who is always called His Father.

B. The Result of the Virgin Birth

The result of the virgin birth was the incarnation. A human nature was conceived, not a person, for the Second Person existed always. With the conception of the human nature the God-man came into existence, and it was a perfect humanity. This means that although the components of humanity were present, it was a sinless human nature, not merely a sanctified human nature. But the incarnation also brought limitation—not any limitation of a moral nature but only those amoral limitations of humanity. In other words, nothing was missing from His humanity which is essential to humanity and nothing was added which was non-human.

II. THE LIFE OF CHRIST

A. Christ Was Anointed by the Spirit

In the New Testament, anointing is mentioned in relation to Christ only in the following passages: Luke 4:18; Acts 4:27; 10:38; Hebrews 1:9. This probably occurred at His baptism, though anointing is not synonymous with baptism. It was not the same as the filling of the Spirit, which Christ experienced from the moment of birth, but anointing did mark off a new phase of His ministry during which the power of the Spirit was manifest publicly through Him. It distinguished the true Christ from all false ones. Anointing, then, had these characteristics in relation to Christ's life and ministry.

1. The anointing of Jesus of Nazareth distinguished Him as the Messiah. Peter referred to this in the prayer which he led after the first persecution of the disciples: "For of a truth against thy holy child Jesus, whom thou hast anointed, both Herod, and Pontius Pilate, with the Gentiles, and the people of Israel, were gathered together" (Acts 4:27). The writer to the Hebrews makes the same point about anointing as marking Jesus off: "Thou hast loved righteousness, and hated iniquity; therefore God, even thy God, hath anointed thee with the oil of gladness above thy fellows" (Heb. 1:9).

2. The act of anointing empowered Jesus for His prophetic ministry. In the synagogue at Nazareth He said: "The Spirit of the Lord is upon me, because he hath anointed me to preach the gospel to the poor . . ." (Luke 4:18).

3. Peter connected Jesus' anointing with His ministry to do good: "How God anointed Jesus of Nazareth with the Holy Ghost and with power: who went about doing good, and healing all that were oppressed of the devil; for God was with him" (Acts 10:38).

B. Christ Was Filled with the Spirit

There are two specific references to the filling in relation to the Lord Jesus Christ. They are (1) Luke 4:1 which says that He was filled with the Spirit after His baptism; and (2) John 3:34 which declares that "God giveth not the Spirit by measure unto him." Although neither of these references specifically states that Christ was filled from the time of His conception or birth, this fact may be inferred from Old Testament prophecies of the Messiah. For instance, Isaiah spoke of the relation between the Holy Spirit and the Messiah in this way: "And the spirit of the Lord shall rest upon him, the spirit of wisdom and understanding, the spirit of counsel and might, the spirit of knowledge and of the fear of the Lord" (Isa. 11:2). In another place Isaiah prophesied concerning God's servant: "Behold my servant, whom

I uphold; mine elect, in whom my soul delighteth; I have put my spirit upon him . . ." (Isa. 42:1) . Verses like these imply that the filling of the Holy Spirit was always the experience of Messiah, and that would mean from the time of His birth.

C. Christ Was Sealed with the Spirit

Christ declared this fact of Himself as recorded in John 6:27. The seal was the mark of His heavenly origin and the proof of His divine sonship.

D. Christ Was Led by the Spirit

After His baptism Christ was led by the Spirit into the wilderness for the temptation by Satan (Luke 4:1) . His continuous obedience to the guidance of the Spirit enabled Him to do always the things that pleased the Father (John 8:29) .

E. Christ Rejoiced in the Spirit

In Luke 10:21 it is recorded that Christ rejoiced in the Holy Spirit (the Greek text adds "Holy." See ASV) . This was part of the fruit of the Spirit which abounded in Him.

F. Christ Was Empowered by the Spirit

In the controversy with the Pharisees which led to their committing the unpardonable sin, Christ made it clear that He was casting out demons by the power of the Spirit (Matt. 12:28) . The question arises, Were all of His miracles performed in the power of the Spirit? Or stated another way, Was Christ dependent on the power of the Spirit to perform miracles during His earthly ministry? In addition to the instance in Matthew 12, the record in Luke 4:14-15, 18 also shows that His power to give sight to the blind and deliverance to the bruised was that of the Spirit. This would show that He performed numerous miracles in the power of the Spirit.

On the other hand, some of His miracles were performed in His own power. The healing of the woman with the issue of blood was the result of His own power (Mark 5:30) . The miracle of the healing of the paralytic who was let down through the tiling of the roof by his friends is attributed to the "power of the Lord" (Luke 5:17 ff.) . The mass healing of the multitude after the choosing of the disciples was the result of His own power (Luke

6:19). When our Lord was accosted in the garden of Gethsemane, He replied in answer to the question of the crowd as to His identity, "I am" (John 18:6). At this they fell to the ground, probably as a result of a momentary flash of His own power.

Thus we have clear statements that certain of His miracles were done in the power of the Spirit and certain in His own power. Therefore, a correct statement of this matter would be as follows: Christ did not have to perform miracles in the power of the Spirit, but He did so on certain occasions; in some instances He clearly used His own power.

What is the significance of these facts concerning the Spirit's working in the life and ministry of our Lord?

1. In the first place the ministry of the Spirit was related to the development of Christ's human nature. Although His divine nature was immutable, His human nature was subject to development. For example, He grew in wisdom (Luke 2:52) and He learned obedience (Heb. 5:8). This development was in no way connected with overcoming sin, for He knew no sin, nor was it the development of a body which had been contaminated by sin. But there was genuine growth, and this was empowered by the Spirit.

2. The fact that Christ depended on the power of the Spirit emphasizes the depth of His condescension. That the God-man should have to be dependent on the ministry of the Spirit to Him shows something of the limitations of humanity.

3. All this is a vivid reminder of the believer's need of the Holy Spirit in his life. If the Lord of glory did not do without the ministry of the Spirit, how can sinners, though redeemed, live independently of His power? If He depended, so must I.

III. THE DEATH OF CHRIST

The only direct Scripture reference which might teach that the Holy Spirit played a part in the death of Christ is Hebrews 9:14: "How much more shall the blood of Christ, who through the eternal Spirit offered himself without spot to God, purge your conscience from dead works to serve the living God?" Of course, one may infer that if the Holy Spirit sustained Him in life, He also sustained Him in the sufferings of death. But Hebrews 9:14 is the only direct reference.

The evidence that this *is* a reference to the Holy Spirit is as follows:

(1) The lack of the article (literally, through eternal spirit) points to the Holy Spirit just as the lack of the article in Hebrews 1:1 is a very unique way of pointing to Christ.

(2) If this is not a reference to the Holy Spirit, then the picture is of the divine nature offering up the human nature, whereas the truth is that the whole person of Christ offered Himself.

(3) Theologically it is reasonable to expect that the Spirit had a part in Christ's death as He had in His life.

The evidence that this *is not* a reference to the Holy Spirit but rather to Christ's eternal spirit within Himself is as follows:

(1) The lack of the article would more naturally point to other than the Holy Spirit, since the designation Holy Spirit usually includes the article.

(2) If this is a reference to Christ's eternal spirit, then it is not a reference to the divine nature offering up the human nature, but to the entire person offering up Himself by the action of the highest power within Himself. This is Christ's own divine spirit (proved by the adjective "eternal") which makes the offering of the whole person of Christ.

Thus the evidence is fairly equally balanced, making a definite conclusion difficult. Whether it is a reference to the Holy Spirit or Christ's spirit, what is involved in this offering will remain an inscrutable mystery.

IV. THE RESURRECTION OF CHRIST

Three passages bear upon the subject of the Spirit's relation to the resurrection of Christ.

A. Romans 8:11

The first reference is Romans 8:11: "But if the Spirit of him that raised up Jesus from the dead dwell in you, he that raised up Christ from the dead shall also quicken your mortal bodies by his Spirit that dwelleth in you." However, a close examination of the verse shows that the "he" that raised up Jesus from the dead is God, not the Holy Spirit. The Holy Spirit's indwelling of the believer is a guarantee of the believer's future resurrection, but actually the verse does not teach that the Spirit had a part in the resurrection of Christ.

B. Romans 1:4

The second relevant verse is Romans 1:4: "And declared to be
the Son of God with power, according to the spirit of holiness,
by the resurrection from the dead." But again this is a doubtful
piece of evidence, since it is not clear that "spirit of holiness" is
a reference to the Holy Spirit. The parallelism in the passage—
"according to the flesh" (v. 3) and "according to the spirit of
holiness" (v. 4)—seems to dictate that this is not a reference to
the Holy Spirit but to Christ's own divine spirit. The problem
may be further studied in good commentaries, but at best it is a
dubious reference to the Holy Spirit.

Further, even if this is a reference to the Holy Spirit, verse 4
is not a clear reference to the resurrection of Christ but more
probably to the resurrection of dead persons (i.e., those whom
Christ raised from the dead during His earthly ministry and
whose resurrection proved His deity). The form is plural and
would seem to point to this interpretation. (However, some, like
Sanday in the *International Critical Commentary*, say that the
plural "dead ones" in connection with "resurrection" means a
"dead-rising" and therefore could refer to Christ's rising from
the dead.)

C. I Peter 3:18

The third verse is I Peter 3:18: "For Christ also hath once
suffered for sins, the just for the unjust, that he might bring us
to God, being put to death in the flesh, but quickened by the
Spirit." Although conceivably "in the Spirit" (*pneumati*) could
be locative and thus mean that He was made alive in His own
spirit, it very likely is instrumental and means that Christ was
made alive by the Spirit. Thus it would be a reference to the
Holy Spirit.

But the problem in the verse is not so much whether this is a
clear reference to the Holy Spirit; rather the problem is whether
it is a reference to the Spirit's work in relation to Christ's resurrection or to His crucifixion. If it is a reference to the resurrection, then the aorist participle ("quickened") expresses action
subsequent to that of the main verb ("suffered"). The suffering
was at the time of His death; therefore, if "quickened" refers to
the resurrection, that is subsequent action. Now the problem
simply is that unless this verse is an exception, the aorist parti-

ciple never expresses action subsequent to that of the main verb.[1] If, therefore, the aorist participle were to maintain its normal meaning, it would express contemporaneous action, and thus the quickening refers to something that occurred at the same time as the suffering; i.e., a quickening on the cross. What this may have involved of the Spirit's working at the time of Christ's death is difficult to ascertain exactly, but that the Spirit did have a part in an exaltation at the time of the crucifixion seems evident from this verse.

Actually, then I Peter 3:18 is a proof text for Section III above, and we will have to conclude that there is no specific proof for the Spirit's working in relation to the resurrection of Christ.

To sum up: The Holy Spirit is definitely declared to be the agent of the virgin birth of Christ; there are many references to the Spirit's working in the life of Christ during His ministry; there is one reference to a quickening by the Spirit at the time of Christ's death (I Peter 3:18) ; but there are no clear references to indicate that the Spirit had a part in the resurrection of Christ. Of course, insofar as the Trinity is involved, the Holy Spirit is included in all such activities of the Trinity.

[1]A. T. Robertson, A Grammar of the Greek New Testament (New York: Harper & Bros., 1923), pp. 861-64.

8

THE SIN AGAINST THE HOLY SPIRIT

ON SEVERAL OCCASIONS the Lord Jesus was accused of casting out demons through the power of the prince of the demons, Satan. It happened near Capernaum (Matt. 9:34) ; it happened in Judea or Perea (Luke 11:14-23) ; but the classic instance was in Galilee as recorded in Matthew 12:22-32 and Mark 3:22-30.

I. THE CONTROVERSY CONCERNING THE SIN

A. The Cause of the Controversy (Matt. 12:22-23)

The controversy arose because the Lord healed a man. The man was a very difficult case, for he was blind and dumb (which likely included deafness) —all caused by demon possession. Such a combination of ills would make his case impossible for an exorcist to do anything about, since he could not even communicate with a deaf, dumb, and blind man. Thus the healing of the man was the more outstanding, and all of his maladies were cured at once. As a result, the people were amazed and expressed the conviction that Jesus was the Son of David. By so saying they were acknowledging Him as the Messiah. It was this that brought out the reaction of the Pharisees.

B. The Charge in the Controversy (Matt. 12:24-29)

So the Pharisees hurled their accusation at Jesus. It was simply this: Satan is obliging his friend Jesus by withdrawing demons from men; who then would want to follow a person who is a friend of Satan as Jesus obviously is?

The Lord's reply was in three parts (vv. 25-29) : (1) A kingdom or house which is divided against itself cannot stand. In other words, Satan would not destroy his own kingdom (though conceivably he might allow demons to be cast out by Jewish exorcists to confuse, but this would not be the same kind of basic rift which Jesus' casting out demons was making) . (2) The charge of diabolic agency in Jesus' case was absurd since the Pharisees recognized that the Jewish exorcists did not cast out demons by the power of Satan. All such exorcists were not pretenders and apparently had success in some instances, but that they were not always successful is evident from the number of people who came to Jesus to be freed of demons. (3) The only logical conclusions to be reached from these facts is that the kingdom of God had come, and the very fact that Christ had begun to bind Satan by taking his prey from him shows that the kingdom had come (vv. 28-29). And the power by which Christ was doing this was the power of the Spirit of God.

II. THE CHARACTER OF THE SIN

This sin has three characteristics:

1. It was directed against the Holy Spirit (Matt. 12:31-32). The Pharisees had put themselves on the side of Satan by accusing Jesus of being in league with Satan. Their accusation was not simply against Christ, but against the Spirit by whose power Christ was casting out demons. What did the Lord mean, then, when He declared that a sin against the Son of Man is forgivable but not one against the Spirit? He meant that men might have misunderstood His ministry and, while this was deplorable, it was forgivable. But they should for no reason have misunderstood the power of the Spirit, for His power was well known from Old Testament times. They could not misunderstand the power of the Spirit and keep on preferring darkness to light and the works of Satan to those of God and expect to be forgiven.

"But there is such a thing as opposition to divine influence, so persistent and deliberate, because of constant preference of darkness to light, that repentance, and therefore forgiveness, becomes impossible. The efficacy of divine grace remains undiminished, but the sinner has brought himself to such a condition that its operation on himself is excluded. Grace, like bodily food, may be rejected until the power to receive it is lost. Christ warns the Pharisees that they are perilously near to this condition. Against the dictates of reason and justice, they had deliberately treated as diabolical a work of the most surprising mercy and goodness."[1]

2. It was determined by a special situation. Speaking against

[1]Alfred Plummer, *An Exegetical Commentary on the Gospel According to S. Matthew* (London: Scott, 1909), p. 179.

the Holy Spirit is not merely a sin of the tongue. The Pharisees sin was not merely in their words; it was not merely the blasphemy of their lips. Their words revealed their hearts, and it was their desperately wicked condition which was shown by their words. Further, the extreme wickedness of their condition was placed in the brightest light—the personal presence of Christ performing miracles. It was sin committed to His face. The committing of this specific sin required the presence of Christ on the earth; thus to reduplicate it exactly today would be impossible. Nevertheless, to show the same wickedness of heart in rejection of the power of God is not only possible but actually happens every day. Attributing the works of the Spirit of God to Satan was the unpardonable sin in Jesus' day, and rejecting the evidences of His power in any day is also an unpardonable sin.

3. It was eternally damning to the soul (v. 32). Such rejection— evidence of a hardened heart—can never be forgiven, not because God withdraws His grace but because man withdraws himself from all possible contact with God. Forgiveness under such circumstances will never come in this age and therefore will never come in any age, since man's eternal destiny is determined in this present life.

III. THE CURE FOR THE SIN

As long as a man has breath he can be forgiven for any sin. Christ Himself made it clear on that occasion that the thing to do was to get on His side (v. 30). In that statement is an invitation even to the Pharisees who so bitterly opposed Him to change sides. It was they, not the Lord, who kept this from happening.

9

COMMON GRACE

I. DEFINITION

COMMON GRACE is the unmerited favor of God toward all men displayed in His general care for them. Common grace is displayed in three circles of activity.

First, there is the general providential work of God in the world. His work of sustaining, for instance, is an example of this. The sending of rain and fruitful seasons is another example.

Second, common grace is displayed in another circle (somewhat narrower than the first) in the restraint of sin. This is particularly the work of the Spirit, though other persons of the Godhead are involved and they use various means.

Third, there is another ministry of the Spirit in John 16:7-11, which is the narrowest circle of common grace because it is not experienced by everyone. However, it may be classed as an example of common grace simply because it is not something which is done only for the redeemed. On the other hand, this work of the Spirit described in John 16 might be classed separately as a distinct ministry of the Spirit and not as an example of common grace.

II. DESCRIPTION

A. Good Gifts

Without dispute, common grace does consist of God's general work of providing good things for man and the Spirit's restraint of sin in this world (whether or not it includes the ministry of John 16). Although man is totally depraved, he has not been totally forsaken by God. Total depravity means the unmeritoriousness of man in the sight of God, but it does not mean that man is incapable of performing good deeds or receiving and appreciating good things. It simply means that whatever man does he cannot gain merit before God. In the meantime, God continues to give man evidences of His compassion and benignity.

Many of these are natural blessings which God showers upon all men. Some of these blessings which are freely given to all men are:

1. *The goodness of God*—"The Lord is good to all: and his tender mercies are over all his works" (Ps. 145:9).

2. *Sunshine and rain*—". . . for he maketh his sun to rise on the evil and on the good, and sendeth rain on the just and on the unjust" (Matt. 5:45).

3. *The kindness of God*—". . . for he is kind unto the unthankful and to the evil" (Luke 6:35).

4. *Food from the earth*—"Nevertheless he left not himself without witness, in that he did good, and gave us rain from heaven, and fruitful seasons, filling our hearts with food and gladness" (Acts 14:17).

5. *The provision of a Saviour*—". . . we trust in the living God, who is the Saviour of all men, specially of those that believe" (I Tim. 4:10).

All men, not just believers, benefit from these universally bestowed blessings, and God gives them graciously to try to lead the unbeliever to repentance. "Or despisest thou the riches of his goodness and forbearance and long-suffering; not knowing that the goodness of God leadeth thee to repentance?" (Rom. 2:4).

B. Restraint of Sin

God uses many means to restrain sin. Such restraint is the work of the Holy Spirit (Gen. 6:3), although sometimes intermediate means are used—like the prophets (Isa. 63:10-11), or governments (Rom. 13:1-4).

The most detailed passage concerning the restraint of sin is II Thessalonians 2:6-7: "And now ye know what withholdeth that he might be revealed in his time. For the mystery of iniquity doth already work: only he who now letteth will let, until he be taken out of the way." The central problem in these verses is the identification of the restrainer, not the clear fact of restraint. In verse 6 "what withholdeth" is a neuter participle with the neuter article. In verse 7 "he who withholds" is a masculine participle with the masculine article. Further, Paul states that the Thessalonians were acquainted with what it is that restrains (v. 6). Too, it is apparent that the restrainer must be more powerful than Satan who empowers the Man of Sin—otherwise the restrainer could not hold back such evil. The facts of the text, then, are: the restrainer is a principle, the restrainer is a person, the identification is well known to the readers, and the power of the restrainer must be greater than Satan's power.

Most commentators identify the restrainer with the Roman Empire of Paul's day.[1] It is admitted, however, by those who hold this view that the restrainer is not merely the Roman Empire but government in general, since it is quite evident that the Man of Sin did not make his appearance before the end of the Roman Empire. This government view is supported from Paul's own statement that governments are ordained of God for the purpose of restraining evil (Rom. 13:1-7). However, one should recognize that governments do not always fulfill their ordained purpose, and furthermore, no government nor all governments put together would be stronger than Satan himself.

Other suggestions for the identity of the restrainer include Satan (but II Thess. 2:7 precludes this interpretation), some powerful angel (but Jude 9 shows the impotence of the archangel in the face of Satanic opposition), or no positive identification at all. It is sometimes asserted that Paul himself was unsure. But how did the Thessalonians know if Paul did not teach them (II Thess. 2:5-6)? It is more often stated that even though Paul and his readers knew, we who read the letter today cannot know.

Ultimately a decision as to the identity of the restrainer will be made on the basis of answering the question, Who is powerful enough to hold back Satan? The obvious and only answer to that question is that God alone is sufficiently powerful. Therefore, the restrainer must be God. In this view, the neuter in verse 6 would remind us of the power of God in general, and the masculine in verse 7 would point to the person of God. If the restrainer may be more distinctly identified as the Third Person of the Godhead (in line with Gen. 6:3), then the neuter may have been used simply because Spirit is neuter in Greek. The masculine, then, would indicate the personality of the Spirit (as in John 15:26; 16:13-14; Eph. 1:13-14). It is really impossible to identify the restrainer as other than God. Undoubtedly He uses govern-

[1]Cf. George G. Findlay, *Thessalonians, Cambridge Greek Testament* (New York: Cambridge University Press, 1904), pp. 177-79.

58   THE HOLY SPIRIT

ments, elect angels, the Bible, the church, and other means to
restrain evil; but the ultimate power behind such forceful restraint must be the power of God and the person of God. Whether
Paul is specifically referring to the Holy Spirit in this passage
might be debatable, but it does not affect the argument.

In some cases God ceases His restraint of sin and gives men
over to their own ways, with the result that their sin works itself out in complete godlessness and corruption (Rom. 1:24, 26,
28). Even this kind of action on the part of God reminds us
that until He gave men up to such a course of action He was
actively restraining their sin.

C. Proof of the Truth of the Gospel

Another work of the Spirit which may be classed under the
heading of common grace is that of the conviction of sin (John
16:8-11). To be sure, this might be classed under efficacious
grace, but it probably belongs here since His work of conviction
is not always efficacious. Conviction is, however, the smallest
circle of common grace, since it does not affect all men. "The
idea of 'conviction' is complex. It involves the conceptions of
authoritative examination, of unquestionable proof, of decisive
judgment, of punitive power. Whatever the final issue may be,
he who 'convicts' another places the truth of the case in dispute
in a clear light before him, so that it must be seen and acknowledged as truth. He who then rejects the conclusion which the
exposition involves, rejects it with his eyes open and at his peril.
Truth seen as truth carries with it condemnation to all who re-
fuse to welcome it."[2]

This proving the truth of the gospel message is not in general
terms but in the specific areas of sin, righteousness, and judgment. The proof that men are in a state of sin is because "they
believe not on me." The *hoti* ("because") is causal and tells
why men are in sin. "Man is condemned before God not because he is a sinner but because, being in a state of sin, he has
refused to believe in the Saviour and accept His pardon."[3]

Further, the Spirit proves to man the righteousness of Christ,
and this is provable simply because (again causal) Christ rose

[2]B. F. Westcott, *Gospel According to St. John* (London: J. Murray, 1908),
II, 219.
[3]René Pache, *The Person and Work of the Holy Spirit* (Chicago: Moody
Press, 1954), p. 57.

from the dead and returned to the Father. The righteousness is
the righteousness of God exhibited in the person and life of
Christ and is contrasted with all the false concepts of righteousness which the world has. Christ's righteous claims were not
fully vindicated until He was raised and had ascended to a place
of glory and honor. Now the Spirit is able to convince men that
Jesus is the righteous Saviour who will justify those who put their
trust in Him.

Finally, the Spirit gives demonstrable proof of judgment. This
refers to the judgment to come upon all unbelievers, and the
proof of a coming judgment is the already accomplished judgment
of Satan (John 12:31; 16:11). The Holy Spirit persuades men
that the same judgment that overtook Satan will come upon
them if they persist in rejecting Christ.

The order of sin, righteousness, and judgment is a logical one.
Man needs to see his state of sin, then he needs to have proof
of the righteousness of the Saviour who can save him from sin,
and finally he needs to be reminded that if he refuses to receive
that Saviour he will face a certain judgment without hope of
anything but condemnation.

When this proving work of the Holy Spirit accompanies the
preaching of the gospel, all who hear the message will be en-
lightened to the point of understanding that the message is true.
Whether each individual who hears will go on to accept the truth
is not guaranteed by this ministry of the Spirit. Acceptance would
involve the work of regeneration; enlightenment involves only
the giving of demonstrable proof of the truth of the message. But
even that proving is a supernatural work.

III. DEFICIENCIES

Common grace is, of course, deficient in relation to efficacious
grace. While common grace provides good gifts from God to all
men, it does not include the gifts of indwelling and filling of the
Spirit, for instance. Although common grace includes the restraint
of sin, it does not provide regeneration and the grace of sanctification. While common grace shows the validity of the Christian
gospel to men, it does not guarantee that all who hear will accept
Christ as Saviour.

Nevertheless, we should be thankful that God ministers common grace to mankind. This makes it more pleasant to live in

this present evil world. It shows us something of the love, pa-
tience, and long-suffering of God to all men. Because He proves
the truth of our message, it makes it possible for us to preach with
power and conviction. All in all, common grace ought to make
us thankful for His general blessings and dependent on the
Spirit's ministry to undergird our witness.

10

EFFICACIOUS GRACE

I. DEFINITION OF THE DOCTRINE

EFFICACIOUS GRACE is the work of the Holy Spirit which effectively moves men to believe in Jesus Christ as Saviour. It of course involves the whole concept of the sovereign purposes of God, and because of this it is one of the most important doctrines in the Word. It is also a very practical consideration, since rightly understood it brings proper perspective on the whole work of evangelization.

II. DESCRIPTION OF THE DOCTRINE

Efficacious grace by its very definition is effective. This is in contrast to aspects of common grace which can be resisted or at least not acknowledged as from God. Obviously efficacious grace does not exclude the human act of believing. It is the work of the Spirit which moves men to believe; therefore, it may be said that no man is saved against his will. It is not a work apart from human will, but it guarantees effective action upon that will, that moves it without forcing it.

Strictly speaking, efficacious grace is an act and not a process. It may be preceded by any number of processes which lead a man to that point of decision, but the act of making the decision is the work of efficacious grace. Common grace precedes and includes many acts and processes, but when and if effective grace follows, it is the climactic act at the moment of believing.

III. DEFENSE OF THE DOCTRINE

The biblical support of the doctrine is based on the use of the word "call." In only a very few instances does the word convey a general invitation to elect and nonelect alike (cf. Matt. 22:14 and probably Matt. 9:13). The vast majority of occurrences concern the effectual call which leads to salvation. From such verses

as Romans 1:1; 8:28; I Timothy 6:12; II Peter 1:3, 10 it is clear
that the calling is not merely a general invitation but that mysterious yet effectual work of God through the Holy Spirit which
brings man to saving faith in Jesus Christ. To those who are
not called in this effectual sense, the gospel remains foolishness
(I Cor. 1:21-25).

The theological support of the doctrine is vitally connected
with the doctrine of sin. If man is incapable of coming to God,
then he must have effective aid in the form of efficacious grace.
If sin has affected man so that he is a slave to sin and unable to
do that which is pleasing to God for eternal salvation (Rom.
6:20-23), then the salvation of man requires the intervention of
the work of the Spirit in the effectual calling of such a sinner.
Man could not respond to the point of being saved without it,
and the proof of that is the abundant evidence of the downward
path which man takes when he refuses even the ministrations of
common grace (Rom. 1:24-32). The denial of efficacious grace
is usually based on a weak or faulty doctrine of sin.

IV. DIFFICULTIES IN THE DOCTRINE

A. It Is Contrary to Human Effort

It seems as if grace that is effective would involve no human
effort; indeed, it would be contrary to human effort. However,
God has preserved the necessity of believing, and while this is
more a human responsibility than a human effort, it nevertheless is man's part in making efficacious grace effective. Inscrutable
as it may be, it is still true that our salvation depends on our
trusting God to save us (cf. John 6:37).

B. It Is Contrary to Human Responsibility

If efficacious grace is necessary to salvation, and if God alone
can supply such grace, then God cannot hold us responsible if
we reject the Saviour. There are two fallacies in such reasoning.
The first is that no man has a claim on God's grace and, therefore,
no man can question why He gives it to some and not to others.
To contemplate why anyone is saved, not why anyone is lost, is
the only proper approach.

Second, such reasoning forgets that in every case where efficacious grace is not experienced, common grace is received. While

common grace is not sufficient to regenerate, it is sufficient to reveal God and to condemn if it is not received and recognized as from God. For instance, if you offered to give one dollar to a man who you knew needed one hundred dollars and if he rejected your one dollar gift, you would doubtless consider his refusal sufficient grounds for declining to give him further assistance. If, on the other hand, the needy man accepted the one dollar gift gratefully, you might try to give him more. The dollar would be insufficient to meet his need, but if refused it would be sufficient to condemn him. That dollar is like common grace which is not able to save but which is able to condemn, if rejected.

C. It Is Contrary to Fair Play

Again, as in the other two charges, the viewpoint is wrong. Any who would charge God with lack of fairness has forgotten that no man, including himself, has any claim on God and His grace. He has also forgotten that the rejection of the many evidences of common grace bring a verdict of "Condemned!" and free God from any obligation (if He had any at all!) to give further grace.

V. DEMANDS OF THE DOCTRINE

God does not bestow His efficacious grace whimsically and without purpose. His purpose is not only to enlighten, regenerate, and bring a sinner into fellowship with Himself but it is primarily that through this operation He may bring glory to Himself. His purpose is that sinners who have been the recipients of efficacious grace may also "show forth the excellencies of him" who called them "out of the darkness into his marvellous light" (I Peter 2:9-10, ASV). God is glorified through the display of His efficacious grace in the redeemed life. The great doxology for the inscrutable ways of God in Romans 11:33-36 is followed immediately by the earnest appeal to the dedicated life. Grace ought always to motivate to service of the God who has so fully and freely bestowed that grace on undeserving and completely helpless sinners. Grace demands dedication.

11

REGENERATION

I. THE MEANING OF REGENERATION

BIBLICALLY, the word regeneration (*paliggenesia*), is used only twice in the New Testament (Matthew 19:28 and Titus 3:5). In the former reference it is used as a description of the millennium when the Son of Man will sit on the throne of His glory. In the latter instance it is connected with the accomplishing of our salvation by the "washing of regeneration." Since the term means to be born again, other verses which speak of the new birth are relevant to the doctrine.

Theologically, the term means the act of God which imparts eternal life. Erroneously it is often identified with or inclusive of conversion, sanctification, and justification. Those who hold that an infant is regenerated when the water of baptism is placed upon him make regeneration a work preparatory to conversion. In comparison with conversion, regeneration is God's work while conversion is the human counterpart.

II. THE MEANS OF REGENERATION

The Scriptures clearly teach that regeneration is the act of God. Direct statements show this (John 1:13) as well as statements which link regeneration to spiritual resurrection—an act of God alone (John 5:21; Rom. 6:13; II Cor. 5:17). Too, the fact that the new birth is said to be from above shows it is a divine achievement (John 3:3). Particularly it is the work of the Holy Spirit of God (John 3:3-7; Titus 3:5). A proper concept of sin and its total ravages reinforces the conclusion that regeneration must be of God and cannot be accomplished by man. Thus the true means of regeneration is the work of the Spirit in effecting a new birth in man.

Faith is not the means of regeneration, though it is the human requirement which when met enables the Spirit to bring about the new birth. Though faith is closely associated with the

64

new birth, the two ideas are distinct, the one being the human responsibility and channel and the other the work of God. The two occur simultaneously, the attempt to place regeneration before faith on the grounds that an unregenerate man cannot believe being merely academic but in no sense chronological.

Although the Word of God is also closely associated with regeneration, it is not strictly the means either (cf. I Peter 1:23; James 1:18). The Word of God is necessary that man may have proper content to his faith and that he may know what he must believe. Peter and James, by including the reference to the Word of God in connection with regeneration, simply show that the Word of God (like faith) is involved in the whole process whereby God gives men the new birth.

Even efficacious grace does not effect regeneration. It is simultaneous with the act of being born again and necessary to it, but it is not the same. Regeneration is the act of God which effects the new birth, and although the antecedents leading up to it may involve a long time and many processes, the act of being born again itself is instantaneous and of God alone.

III. THE FEATURES OF REGENERATION

A. It Is Instantaneous

As indicated, regeneration is not a process, though its antecedents may be. In other words, there may be many factors and circumstances which lead to a man's conversion, but the actual work of being born again happens instantaneously. This is proved by the aorist tenses which are used in regeneration passages such as John 1:13 and John 3:3, 5, 7. The aorist tense expresses an event rather than a process and, since it is used for regeneration, we conclude that regeneration is an event and not a process. In other passages concerning regeneration the Greek perfect tense is used (as in I John 2:29; 3:9; 4:7; 5:1, 4, 18). The perfect tense also has the idea of a single, decisive, initial act (like the aorist) but adds the idea of lasting results from that instantaneous act of regeneration.

B. It Is Nonexperiential

The dictionary defines experiential as "derived from, based on, or pertinent to experience." Of course, in the sense that regeneration is pertinent to experience it is experiential. But in the sense that it is not derived from or based on experience it is a nonexperiential work of God. This meaning of nonexperiential (that is, of not being derived from or based on human experience) is quite common in theological usage, and this is the sense in which we say that regeneration is not experiential.

But if regeneration is nonexperiential, then might it not be argued that infants may be regenerated as well as adults? It could be so if it were not for the fact that even though faith is not the means of regeneration it is a requirement which must be met before anyone can be regenerated. Believers are those who are born of the Spirit (John 1:12-13), and of course infants are not believers.

IV. THE FRUIT OF REGENERATION

A. A New Nature

The new birth brings a new nature (II Cor. 5:17). It does not eradicate the old nor does it split the personality. Natures are capacities, and whereas the unregenerate man has only the capacity to serve sin (Rom. 6:20), the new nature brings the capacity to serve righteousness (Rom. 6:18). This also makes it possible for the individual to be controlled by the Spirit of God. The regenerate man walks by the Spirit, is led by the Spirit, and can be filled with the Spirit (Rom. 8:4; Gal. 5:16; Rom. 8:14; Eph. 5:18). He is not made perfect, but he does have the new capacity to please God and to grow into the image of Christ by means of the new birth.

B. A NEW LIFE

The new nature will bear fruit in a new life. In passages such as I John 2:29; 3:9; 4:7; 5:1, 4, 18 the abiding results of regeneration are doing righteousness, not committing sin, loving one another, believing that Jesus is the Christ, and overcoming the world. These fruits of the new birth are a vivid reminder that although a man is completely passive in the act of the new birth, the results of that new birth involve far-reaching activity. He must walk in newness of life, bearing the image and manifesting the likeness of the family of God into which he has been born.

12

THE INDWELLING OF THE SPIRIT

THE INDWELLING MINISTRY of the Spirit is the heart of the distinctiveness of the Spirit's work in this Church Age. It is also the center of our Lord's promises to His disciples concerning the ministry of the Spirit after His departure from earth. Too, the doctrine of the indwelling is foundational to the other ministries the Spirit performs today.

I. THE PERSONS WHO ARE INDWELT

All Christians and only Christians are indwelt by the Holy Spirit in this age. This was not always well known by the church, for Paul had to remind believers in the early days that this was a fact (I Cor. 3:16; 6:19) just as it is necessary to instruct believers today of its truth. Nevertheless, the truth of the Spirit's indwelling does not depend on the realization of it. It is proved in four ways.

A. Sinning Christians Are Said to Possess the Holy Spirit

The well-known statement on indwelling in I Corinthians 6:19 was addressed to a very mixed multitude of believers in Corinth. Many were carnal. One brother (note that he was a Christian in Paul's judgment, I Cor. 5:5b) was living in gross sin. Many were at legal swords' points with each other (I Cor. 6). But without exception they were all addressed as those possessing the Holy Spirit. Indeed, their being indwelt by Him was made the basis for Paul's exhortation for good behavior.

B. The Holy Spirit Is a Gift

Many passages teach this (John 7:37-39; Acts 11:17; Rom. 5:5; I Cor. 2:12; II Cor. 5:5). In none of them is the gift said to be given discriminately but rather to all believers. By the nature of a gift this would be expected, for a gift is not a reward and no merit is involved in its being given. Therefore, one would expect that no distinctions would be involved, as indeed they are not according to these many verses.

C. The Absence of the Holy Spirit Is an Evidence of an Unsaved Condition

Paul very emphatically declares: "Now if any man have not the Spirit of Christ, he is none of his" (Rom. 8:9b). In giving his own judgment as to the spiritual condition of the apostates in the churches, Jude says in no uncertain terms: "These be they who separate themselves, sensual, having not the Spirit" (Jude 19). The word translated *sensual* in this verse is the same word translated *natural* in I Corinthians 2:14, another verse describing the unsaved man in terms of his lack of comprehension of any of the ministries of the Spirit. Thus it is clear from these three verses that since the absence of the Spirit is an evidence of an unsaved state, the presence of the Spirit is the gift of God to every believer.

D. The Universal Indwelling of the Father and of Christ Are Inseparably Linked with the Universal Indwelling of the Spirit

The Holy Spirit is the one who reveals to the Christian the indwelling of the Father in him. "And he that keepeth his commandments dwelleth in him, and he in him. And hereby we know that he abideth in us, by the Spirit which he hath given us" (I John 3:24). Thus the knowledge of the indwelling of the Father is dependent on the ministry of the Spirit, which is not restricted but which operates in all believers.

Furthermore, knowing that Christ dwells within us is dependent on the coming of the Spirit. It is the Spirit who will make known Christ's presence (John 14:17-20) and who will glorify and teach of Christ (John 16:13-15). Christ is definitely said to indwell all believers (Col. 3:11); therefore, it is reasonable to conclude that the Spirit also indwells all believers so that the indwelling of Christ may be known by all. And this reasonable conclusion is confirmed by the proofs cited above.

II. THE PERMANENCE OF THE INDWELLING

Does the Spirit abide permanently within the believer or is there some sin which would cause Him to depart? Some Christians sincerely believe that although the Spirit is given as a gift at conversion, He will withdraw Himself when certain sin is committed. However, the Lord said that He would abide forever (John 14:16). Furthermore, if sin could cause His removal, then that same sin must also cause the person who committed it to become unsaved again, for the absence of the Spirit is evidence of an unsaved condition. Thus the security of the believer and the permanent indwelling of the Spirit are truths that are inseparably linked together.

It is true, nevertheless, that sin affects the ministry of the Spirit to the believer. However, it does not affect His indwelling. Sin grieves the Spirit (Eph. 4:30) and causes the power of His indwelling, but not the fact of it, to be diminished. It is the filling of the Spirit (to be discussed later), not the indwelling of the Spirit that is affected by sin.

III. THE PERCEPTION OF THE INDWELLING

Even though the indwelling of the Spirit is nonexperiential in the sense that it is not dependent on our experience, it is important that the Christian perceives that it is a fact, in order to bring into his life certain subsequent experiences of fellowship and power. The Lord promised that His followers would know (John 14:17, 20) that the Spirit indwells. How, then, can we know?

There are two possible avenues of evidence—the Word and experience. Of the two, there is no question that the Word is the better, for experience can be lacking or deceiving. Indeed, we may say that the only sure proof of the indwelling of the Spirit in the lives of believers is that the Word of God declares that it is so (I Cor. 6:19). "May we, therefore, learn to believe that the Spirit is in us, children of God, simply because the Bible tells us so. Then, when we have believed (and not before), we shall see this Spirit bring forth in our hearts that love, joy and peace which we had hitherto sought in vain (Gal. 5:22-23)."[1]

Experience may or may not confirm the fact of indwelling. If there is sin in the life, then there will be few if any experiences of power, for sin hinders the working of the Spirit and may lead to the erroneous conclusion that the Spirit does not even dwell within. Too, in the normal process of Christian growth there may be periods of slow but steady and unspectacular growth during which there will be no unusual demonstrations of the

[1]René Pache, *The Person and Work of the Holy Spirit* (Chicago: Moody Press, 1954), p. 104.

70 THE HOLY SPIRIT

Spirit's power. This should never be diagnosed as absence of in-dwelling. Experience, then, is never a safe and certain test.

IV. THE PROBLEMS INVOLVED IN INDWELLING

A. Is Obedience a Condition for Indwelling (Acts 5:32)?

Acts 5:32 seems to indicate that obedience is a condition for receiving the Spirit: "And we are his witnesses of these things; and so is also the Holy Ghost, whom God hath given to them that obey him." Is the Spirit then given only to certain believers? Before coming to such a conclusion, let us see what the required obedience is.

The setting of Peter's message on this occasion leaves no doubt that he was referring to obedience of faith in Christ. He was not addressing Christians and offering to some of them who would obey a special gift of the Spirit. He was addressing the unbe-lieving Sanhedrin and stipulating the condition for becoming a Christian in terms of obeying by believing in Jesus as Messiah. In the very next chapter the same expression is used to describe the conversion of a number of the priests who were said to have been "obedient to the faith" (Acts 6:7). The requirement of salvation is stated similarly in Hebrews 5:9: "And being made perfect, he became the author of eternal salvation unto all them that obey him." Likewise Paul stated the purpose of his apostle-ship and mission as "for obedience to the faith among all nations, for his name" (Rom. 1:5). Thus obedience is a condition for receiving the indwelling of the Holy Spirit, but it is the obedience of faith in Christ as Saviour.

B. Are There Not Illustrations of the Temporary Nature of Indwelling?

Although we have discussed the matter of the permanence of the indwelling of the Spirit, certain verses are alleged to teach that He may be withdrawn. It is recorded of Saul that the Spirit departed from him (I Sam. 16:14), and David prayed that the Spirit be not taken from him (Ps. 51:11). In addition, a verse in the Gospels might seem to indicate that the Spirit may be given and taken away repeatedly (Luke 11:13). However, it must be recognized that all these instances were pre-Pentecostal. And that is very important, for it is not until Pentecost that we

THE INDWELLING OF THE SPIRIT

can expect any normalcy in the operation of the Spirit in this age. After all, the Lord Himself recognized the pre- and post-Pentecostal difference as late as the upper room discourse where the majority of the promises concerning the coming and ministry of the Spirit were given. Therefore, even if the Spirit was removed from the lives of people before Pentecost, the fact that this happened before Pentecost rules out carrying over such experience into the post-Pentecost era.

C. Does Not the Delay in the Giving of the Spirit to the Samaritans Prove That It is Subsequent to Salvation (Acts 8:14-17)?

That there was a delay in the giving of the Spirit to the Samaritans who had believed is beyond question. Was there any reason for this delay, or does it signify that the indwelling of the Spirit comes subsequent to salvation? Some say that this was a filling of the Spirit, but it clearly was not, and such an answer really avoids the problem. Others say that this was different because the Samaritans were the first non-Jewish group to be taken into the church. This is half true but the Samaritans were also partly Jewish. However, when the Spirit was given to Gentiles, it happened at the moment of believing (Acts 10:44), making that, if anything, the norm for non-Jewish believers.

The best explanation of this delay in Samaria seems to lie in the schismatic nature of the Samaritan religion. Because the Samaritans had their own worship, which was a rival to the Jewish worship in Jerusalem, it was necessary to prove to them that their new faith was not to be set up as a rival to the new faith that had taken root in Jerusalem. And the best way for God to show the Samaritan believers that they belonged to the same faith and group as Jerusalem believers (and contrariwise, the best way to show the Jerusalem leaders that the Samaritans were genuinely saved) was to delay the giving of the Spirit until Peter and John came from Jerusalem to Samaria. There could be no doubt then that this was one and the same faith and that they all belonged together in the Body of Christ. This delay in the giving of the Spirit saved the early church from having two mother churches— one in Jerusalem and one in Samaria—early in her history. It preserved the unity of the church in this early stage.

72   THE HOLY SPIRIT

D. Does Not Acts 19:1-6 Show That the Indwelling Is Subsequent to Salvation?

When Paul arrived in Ephesus on the third missionary journey he discovered a group of twelve disciples of John the Baptist. He asked them if they had received the Holy Spirit when they believed John's message. When they confessed complete ignorance of the Spirit, Paul explained to them the preparatory ministry of John in relation to Christ. When they heard and understood the difference, they believed and were baptized in the name of Christ, at which time they did receive the Spirit. Whatever problem might seem to be raised by the fact that these men did not receive the Spirit under the preaching of John is solved by remembering that they did not become believers in Christ until Paul preached to them at Ephesus. They were not believers in Jesus by believing John's message, for they obviously did not even understand the meaning of John's message and baptism (vv. 3-4) to say nothing of the Christian message. But when they did understand and believe in Jesus, then they received the Spirit immediately.

The only exception to the normal procedure of giving the Spirit at the time of conversion was the experience of the Samaritans, whose case was peculiar and unique. The pattern and particularly the Gentile pattern was established and followed from the time of Cornelius on, so that every Christian is indwelt permanently when he believes.

E. What Is the Relation of the Anointing of the Spirit to Indwelling?

Anointing with the holy oil was a solemn matter in the Old Testament (Exodus 30:32-33). When a person or thing was anointed, it became holy and sacrosanct (Exodus 30:22-33). It was associated with the Holy Spirit and connected with equipping for service (I Sam. 10:1, 9; Zech. 4:1-14). In the New Testament a spiritual anointing is referred to only in Luke 4:18; Acts 4:27; 10:38; II Corinthians 1:21; I John 2:20, 27; and Hebrews 1:9. All these references except those in II Corinthians and I John relate to Christ. As far as the believer is concerned, the remaining three references teach:

1. That God does the anointing.

2. That it is not a repeated act on His part (both II Cor. 1:21 and I John 2:27 use the aorist tense).

3. That the anointing, though not repeated, abides (note the present tense of "abide" in I John 2:27).

Thus the anointing seems to be very closely related to the indwelling in that it occurs once and upon all believers without respect to their spiritual condition, and that it remains. In these characteristics it is similar to the indwelling of the Spirit.

The difference between anointing and indwelling seems to lie in their distinct purposes. The indwelling brings the presence of God into the life of the believer. The anointing, as far as the believer is concerned, is that he might be taught (I John 2:20, 27). Actually this seems to be the only purpose specified in the believer's case. However, if one may use the example of the anointing of Christ and of Old Testament priests, then another purpose emerges—that of service. Anointing in these cases was to set apart for service. But teaching is the only ministry specified in relation to the anointing of the believer. Of course, as in the case of other ministries of the Spirit, the full experience of the anointing depends on being filled with the Spirit.

13

THE BAPTIZING WORK OF THE HOLY SPIRIT

I. CONFUSION CONCERNING THE BAPTIZING WORK

THIS (and perhaps the temporary character of certain spiritual gifts) is the most confusing aspect of the entire doctrine of the Holy Spirit. Confusion of this sort is most difficult to combat since it is bound up with experience; and it is always difficult, if not impossible, to show that experience is wrong—especially if the doctrine might be stretched to cover the experience! Furthermore, many believers have a sincere hunger to know and experience the power of God; therefore, any experience like the baptism of the Spirit which might contribute to bringing this power is off limits to academic discussion.

A. Reasons for the Confusion

1. There is an improper understanding of the distinctiveness of the church to this age. This leads to confusion about the baptizing work of the Spirit which forms the church. If one believes that the church began with Abraham or with John the Baptist, then it will be difficult to understand the distinctiveness of the baptism of the Spirit to this age and what that baptism accomplishes.

2. There is an overbalance on the doctrine of water baptism which often obscures the doctrine of Spirit baptism. If the two truths are not distinguished it is usually the truth of Spirit baptism that is lost, for it is regarded simply as another way of talking about water baptism.

3. The association of baptism with the gift of tongues multiplies confusion. Of course, if speaking with tongues is the evidence of the baptism of the Spirit, then the baptism does not come at the time of salvation nor is it experienced by all Christians. Some, to justify the association of baptism with tongues, attempt to make a distinction between the baptism *by* the Spirit of I Corin-

thians 12:13, which places one into the Body of Christ, and the baptism *with* the Spirit of Acts 1:5, which brings tongues. However, in both verses the baptism is described as *en pneumati,* and it would seem risky at best to build two separate doctrines on exactly the same phrase.

4. Baptism is frequently identified with filling of the Spirit. Sometimes the terms "baptism" and "filling" are confused, while at other times the same error is stated by asserting that the baptism does not come at the time of regeneration but as a subsequent work of grace. Confusion is compounded by the fact that great men like Torrey and Moody were unclear. Torrey taught that a person could or could not be baptized with the Spirit at the moment of regeneration.[1] The baptism as a subsequent work of grace in Moody's life is recounted in his biography.[2] After concluding the account of Mr. Moody's baptism, Torrey comments as follows: "Once he had some teachers at Northfield—fine men, all of them, but they did not believe in a definite baptism with the Holy Ghost for the individual. They believed that every child of God was baptized with the Holy Ghost, and they did not believe in any special baptism with the Holy Ghost for the individual."[3]

B. Results of the Confusion

Such confusion results in misunderstanding and divisions among Christians. But worse than this, a lack of understanding of this doctrine obscures the important truth of our union with Christ, a consequence of which is a lack of any genuine basis for Christian living. If one does not understand the baptizing work of the Spirit, then he cannot understand the only sure basis for holy living. The baptism joins us to Christ and this is the basis for victory.

II. CHARACTERISTICS OF THE BAPTIZING WORK

A. It Is Limited to This Age

The baptizing work of the Spirit is the one work of the Spirit which is not found in any other dispensation. This is proved

[1] R. A. Torrey, *The Baptism with the Holy Spirit,* pp. 13-14.
[2] R. A. Torrey, *Why God Used D. L. Moody* (New York: Fleming H. Revell Co., 1923), pp. 51-55.
[3] *Ibid.,* p. 55.

theologically and biblically. Theologically, the proof is based on I Corinthians 12:13: "For by one Spirit are we all baptized into one body, whether we be Jews or Gentiles, whether we be bond or free; and have been all made to drink into one Spirit." If it is the baptizing work of the Spirit that places a person in the Body of Christ, and if the Body of Christ—because it depends on the resurrection and ascension of Christ—is distinctive to this age, then so is the baptism.

Biblically, the baptizing work is never mentioned as being experienced in the Old Testament or in the days of Christ's earthly ministry. Indeed, after His resurrection and just before His ascension He declared that it was yet future (Acts 1:5). That it first occurred on the day of Pentecost is proved by the fact that the Lord said it would occur "not many days hence," and by the fact that Peter said it happened when he referred to the Pentecost experience in Acts 11:15-17. Although the Spirit will be active in the millennial age, no specific mention of His baptizing work then is given in the Bible. Therefore, we conclude that it is a ministry particular to this age.

B. It Is Universal Among All Believers in This Age

This is proved by three facts. The first is I Corinthians 12:13, particularly in its context. Paul did not say that only the spiritual element at Corinth had been baptized. Neither did he exhort them to be baptized in order to become spiritual (and certainly this would have been an easy solution to the problems in that church if the baptism of the Spirit means filling and enduing with power). He simply stated that all had been baptized with the Spirit (aorist tense).

The second fact is contained in Ephesians 4:5: "One Lord, one faith, one baptism." "One baptism" evidently belongs to the same group as "one Lord" and "one faith"; i.e., all Christians.

The third fact that shows this baptizing work is universal among believers is the lack of exhortations or commands to be baptized anywhere in the New Testament. One would rightly expect such exhortations if the baptism were not experienced by all Christians, but the fact that such exhortations are missing confirms the universal experience of baptism by all believers.

C. It Is Repeated Each Time a Person Is Converted but Is Experienced Only Once by Each Believer

Some teach that the baptizing work of the Spirit was performed only at Pentecost and never again and that when a person is saved he merely partakes of what was done at Pentecost.[4] However, the repetition of the giving of the gift of tongues in the house of Cornelius (Acts 10:46) seems to indicate a fresh work of baptizing on that occasion. Nevertheless, a believer is baptized only once, and that at his conversion. There is no scriptural reference which would indicate that the same person or persons were baptized a second time. Indeed, the aorist tense of I Corinthians 12:13 indicates an unrepeated experience. By contrast, the filling of the Spirit is said to be experienced by the same group on more than one occasion (Acts 2:4; 4:31), and the command to be filled is expressed by a present tense (Eph. 5:18). The once-for-all baptizing of the Spirit places one into the Body of Christ; therefore, if it could be repeated, it would mean that a person could be removed from that Body in order that he could be reinstated into it again by a second baptism. Such a fanciful idea is completely foreign to the Scriptures.

D. It Is a Nonexperiential Work of the Spirit

By this is meant, as in the case of other ministries of God in behalf of the believer, that the baptizing work of the Spirit is not based upon or derived from experience. It happens whether or not the believer is conscious of it. It is not implied, however, that no resultant experience flows from this ministry. Many experiences in the believer's life are the result of being placed in the Body of Christ through the baptizing work of the Spirit, but the baptism itself is nonexperiential.

E. It Is the Work of the Holy Spirit

Mention has already been made of the fact that some consider there are two baptisms which concern the Holy Spirit. Such people base this idea on different translations for the same preposition which is used in the Greek text. That preposition is *en*. It can be translated *in* or *with* (this is the dative use of it) and that is the way those who see two baptisms translate it in Acts 1:5: ". . . but ye shall be baptized with [or in] the Holy Ghost not

[4]E.g., James M. Gray in D. H. Dolman, *Simple Talks on the Holy Spirit* (New York: Fleming H. Revell Co., 1927), p. 6.

many days hence." The preposition can also be translated *by*
(this is the instrumental use of it) and that is the way it is translated in I Corinthians 12:13: "For by one Spirit we are all baptized into one body. . . ."

There is no question that the preposition can be translated
both *in* and *by*. The "by" translation or instrumental use is
clearly seen in such passages as Luke 22:49 ("with the sword")
and Matthew 12:24 ("by Beelzebub"). Those who wish to see
two baptisms do not quarrel over the translation "by" in I Corinthians 12:13, but they do insist that the translation cannot be
"by" in Acts 1:5. If it were, then of course there are not two
baptisms but only one in which the Spirit is the instrument that
does the baptizing. They want Acts 1:5 to mean that Christ is
the one who baptizes into the sphere of the Holy Spirit, but the
sphere into which a Christian is placed is the risen body and
life of Christ (Rom. 6). The sphere is nowhere revealed in
Scripture to be the Holy Spirit (unless it be this different translation of Acts 1:5), but is revealed to be Christ—just as I Corinthians 12:13 teaches. The instrument that places the believer
into that sphere of the risen body of Christ is the Holy Spirit,
and this is what is taught in both Acts 1:5 and I Corinthians 12:
13. Of course, there is a sense in which, being in the Body of
Christ, we participate in the ministries of the Spirit. This is
doubtless what Paul means by his statement that we "have been
all made to drink into one Spirit" (I Cor. 12:13*b*). But the
chief emphasis is on the Spirit as the agent of baptism who
places us in the Body of Christ.

III. CONSEQUENCES OF THE BAPTIZING WORK

A. The Baptism of the Spirit Makes Us Members of the Body of Christ

This is the primary revelation concerning the result of being
baptized by the Spirit (I Cor. 12:13). This means a resurrection
position with its consequent requirement of living accordingly.
In this context the particular emphasis is on the proper exercise
of gifts and the necessity for keeping the unity of the Body. The
same truth is emphasized in connection with the mention of the
one baptism in Ephesians 4:5, for the context (vv. 3, 6) speaks
of the need for unity among members of that Body. Likewise, in

Galatians 3:27, where being baptized into Christ is mentioned by Paul, the oneness of the Body of Christ is associated in the immediate context. Thus three of the principal passages concerning the baptizing work of the Spirit link its practical outworking to the unity of believers.

B. The Baptism of the Spirit Effects the Union with Christ in His Death unto the Sin Nature

The baptizing work is the means of actualizing our co-crucifixion with Christ (Col. 2:12 and especially Rom. 6:1-10). Being associated by baptism into His death, burial, and resurrection is the basis for the crucifixion of the believer's sin nature and his victory over sin.

Obviously water baptism could not accomplish this union with Christ in His death and resurrection, but equally obvious is the fact that there must be some connection between the baptism by the Spirit and baptism by water. The connection is simply that water baptism is the outward picturing of what the Spirit does in the heart.

C. The Baptism of the Spirit Does Not Necessarily Mean a Special Enduement with Power

The baptism by the Spirit places us in a position in Christ which enables us to receive power, but the act of baptizing does not in itself guarantee that power will be experienced or displayed in the life. The Corinthians who were all baptized fell far short of being sterling displays of God's power in their lives. They were baptized but carnal. No pastor would want to stay long in a church like that at Corinth even though all his members had received the baptism. The Galatians, too, had been baptized and had put on Christ (3:27), but they were actually turning away from the true gospel (1:6) and returning to weak and beggarly elements (4:9). As far as the occurrences of the baptism with the Spirit in Acts are concerned, the power connected with them is that of bringing men to Christ (Acts 2:41; 10:47; 19:5). But even this could not be absolutely guaranteed, for baptism alone apparently is not an assured demonstration of power. To experience what the baptism does accomplish requires the filling of the Spirit.

14

THE SEALING WITH THE SPIRIT

I. THE AGENT OF THE SEALING

THE SEALING MINISTRY of the Holy Spirit is mentioned in the following passages: II Corinthians 1:22; Ephesians 1:13 and 4:30. An additional reference (John 6:27) reveals that Christ was sealed by the Father, but the sealing ministry of the Spirit in relation to the believer is confined to the three passages mentioned.

According to II Corinthians 1:22 it is God who seals the believer. He is the agent, and this is in harmony with what is revealed about the Father's sealing the Son in John 6:27.

II. THE SPHERE OF THE SEALING

The Holy Spirit is the seal. The believer is sealed with or in the Spirit. In Ephesians 1:13 there is no preposition expressed; rather, the phrase "with that Holy Spirit of promise" translates the simple phrase *to pneumati* without a preposition. This is probably to be understood as a locative of sphere. In Ephesians 4:30 the preposition *en* is expressed. This could be understood as meaning "by"—that is, instrumental—or it could be understood as a locative just as in 1:13. This locative sense is undoubtedly better, since God is specifically revealed as the agent of sealing, not the Spirit, which interpretation would be required if 4:30 were understood as instrumental. For instance, when we say that something is sealed in wax, we mean that the substance of the seal is wax and that someone outside did the sealing. When the Scriptures declare that the Christian is sealed with the Spirit, they mean that He is the substance of the seal itself, and God is the outside person who does the sealing.

III. THE EXTENT OF THE SEALING

The Spirit is the seal for all believers. This is proved in three ways.

First, it is proved by the Scripture recorded in II Corinthians 1:22, which declares no exception to those who are sealed. Indeed, in the light of the carnal state of the Corinthian church, the fact that Paul makes no exception—which he could easily and legitimately have done—is proof that no believer is excepted from the sealing.

Second, it should be noted that the Scriptures nowhere exhort any believer to be sealed. This would imply strongly that it is a universal experience, since it need not be sought by any. If it were not universal, then one would expect to find at least one, if not numerous, exhortations to be sealed, as is the case, for instance, with the filling of the Spirit.

Third, in Ephesians 4:30 the fact that these believers were sealed is made the basis for the exhortation not to grieve the Spirit. Therefore, it is natural to assume that the sealing is universal, otherwise the exhortation not to grieve would lose much of its force.

IV. THE MOMENT OF THE SEALING

The believer is sealed the moment he receives Christ as Saviour Ephesians 1:13 is misleading in the Authorized Version which reads: ". . . in whom also after that ye believed, ye were sealed with that holy Spirit of promise." Literally, the verse reads: ". . . in whom [Christ] having believed [aorist participle] ye were sealed [aorist passive indicative] with that holy Spirit of promise." The important fact in the verse is not so much the time of sealing as the cause. Hearing and believing are necessary to the sealing of the Spirit. In other words, the believing is the necessary cause of the sealing which occurs at the same time. The order in this verse is not chronological though it is logical. We are sealed in order to become His. It is not that we are sealed subsequently to becoming His by faith.

V. THE INTENT OF THE SEALING

In the concept of sealing are the ideas of ownership, authority, responsibility, but above all and including the other ideas is that of security. The primary meaning of sealing is security, and therefore the intent of God's sealing the Christian is to guarantee to him his security. This includes:

1. The certainty of possession by God.
2. The certainty of the promise of His salvation, for there is no

power greater than God who could break the seal, and God Himself has promised never to break it.

3. The certainty of His purpose to keep us until the day of redemption.

Something that is sealed is secure. Something that is sealed by God is as secure as God's promise, and in the case of the believer His promise is to keep that believer until the day of redemption when he shall be fully and forever God's. So sealing is a promise and guarantee of eternal security. It is well to note that this promise in Ephesians 4:30 is made the basis for the exhortation not to grieve the Spirit now by sins of the tongue. The proper doctrine of security never breeds license, though a defective one might.

One of the best earthly illustrations of sealing is a piece of registered mail. When something is registered at the post office, it is sealed until delivered. Actually only two persons can open registered mail—the sender (if it is delivered back to him) and the recipient. In the case of the believer, God is the one who sends him on the way to heaven, and God in heaven is the recipient on his arrival. Therefore, only God can break the seal of our redemption, and He has promised not to do so; and the guarantee of that promise is the presence of the Holy Spirit who is the one in whom we have been sealed by God.

15

SPIRITUAL GIFTS

I. DEFINITION OF GIFTS

A. What Is Meant

THE GREEK WORD for spiritual gift (*charisma*) is obviously related to grace, for *charis* means "grace"; thus a spiritual gift is due to grace. The usage of the word in the New Testament is quite wide, ranging from the gift of salvation (Rom. 6:23) to the gift of God's providential care (II Cor. 1:11, ASV). Usually it is used of the special gifts or abilities given to men by God, and with the exception of I Peter 4:10 the word is used in the New Testament only by Paul. When referring to a gift for service, it seems to include natural talent given at birth (as in Eph. 4 where the emphasis is on gifted men) as well as supernatural talent given at the time of salvation. Thus a spiritual gift may be defined as a God-given ability for service. Its origin is from God; it is an ability, whether natural or supernatural; and it is given for the purpose of service.

B. What Is not Meant

1. A spiritual gift is not primarily a place of service. The gift is the ability, not where that ability is exercised. This is a point that is frequently confused. The gift of pastor, for instance, is often thought of as being equivalent to the pastorate, which is a place of ministry. But of course a teacher may be in a pastorate, and a pastor might be dean of men in a school.

2. A spiritual gift is not primarily a particular age group ministry. There is no spiritual gift of young people's work or children's work. If there were, then there would be a gift of old people's work—a gift which the author has never heard anyone claim to have. Children, young people, and young and older adults all need to benefit from the exercise of the gifts of pastor, teaching, etc.

3. A spiritual gift is not primarily a particular speciality of ministry. There is no gift of writing or Christian education

named in Scripture. The gift of teaching which is named, for instance, may be exercised through writing or through the educational program of the church.

The spiritual gift is the ability, not the place of ministry, nor the persons upon whom it is minstered, nor the speciality of ministry.

II. DISTRIBUTION OF GIFTS

The distribution of gifts is under the sovereign direction of the Holy Spirit. "But all these worketh that one and the selfsame Spirit, dividing to every man severally as he will" (I Cor. 12:11). The Scriptures reveal certain limitations in His method of distribution.

A. Limited as to Agent

As stated, the Spirit is the agent who gives gifts. Man can have a part in developing them, but the ultimate source of all spiritual gifts is the Spirit.

B. Limited as to Extent

It is obvious that no one person has all the spiritual gifts, but it is equally true that every Christian can have and exercise several gifts (I Peter 4:10). Too, all spiritual gifts do not have to appear in every congregation if they do not reside in every Christian.

C. Limited as to Time

If every Christian does not have all the gifts, then it might be true that every generation does not have all the gifts. Indeed, the Scriptures teach that the Spirit has not given all the gifts to every generation. There were foundation gifts of apostles and prophets (Eph. 2:20), which gifts do not appear in the periods of building the superstructure of the church. Those who were contemporary with Christ experienced certain miraculous gifts of the Spirit which were not experienced by the generation which followed Him (Heb. 2:3-4). Actually, it is no argument to say that every gift must appear in every generation of the history of the church so that no generation will be slighted. If a gift is given once, it is given to the entire church. For instance, the gift of apostleship which was given to Saul of Tarsus is a gift to the entire church in all generations. We still profit today from that gift given once in the first century.

III. DEVELOPMENT OF GIFTS

Although the Spirit is the source of spiritual gifts, the believer may have a part in the development of his gifts. He may be ambitious in relation to his own gifts to see that they are properly developed and that he is doing all he can for the Lord (I Cor. 12:31). To covet the better gifts is not a matter of sitting down and conjuring up enough faith to be able to receive them out of the blue. It is a matter of diligent self-preparation. For instance, if one covets the gift of teaching, he will undoubtedly have to spend many years developing that gift. The Holy Spirit is sovereign in the giving of gifts, but in the development of them He works through human beings with their desires, limitations, ambitions, and the like.

IV. DESCRIPTION OF GIFTS

A. Apostleship (Eph. 4:11; I Cor. 12:28)

Apostleship can have both a general and a limited meaning. In a general sense the word means one who is sent, or a messenger. The Latin equivalent is the word missionary. In a general sense every Christian is a missionary or an apostle, because he has been sent into this world for a testimony. Epaphroditus is an illustration, for the word "apostle" is used to describe him ("but your messenger," Phil. 2:25). However, in the specialized sense of the gift of apostleship it refers to the Twelve (and perhaps a few others like Paul and Barnabas, Acts 14:14). They were the leaders who laid the foundation of the church and they were accredited by special signs (Eph. 2:20). Since this was a gift that belonged to the earliest period of the history of the church when her foundation was being laid, the need for the gift has ceased and apparently the giving of it has too. "And are built upon the foundation of the apostles and prophets, Jesus Christ himself being the chief corner stone" (Eph. 2:20).

B. Prophecy (Rom. 12:6; I Cor. 12:10; 14:1-40; Eph. 4:11)

This word also is used in both a general and a limited sense. In a general sense it means to preach; thus, generally speaking, preaching is prophesying, and the preacher is a prophet in that he speaks the message from God. But the gift of prophecy included receiving a message directly from God through special revelation, being guided in declaring it to the people, and having it authenticated in some way by God Himself. The content of that message may have included telling the future (which is what we normally think of as prophesying), but it also included revelation from God concerning the present.

This too was a gift limited in its need and use, for it was needed during the writing of the New Testament and its usefulness ceased when the books were completed. God's message then was contained in written form, and no new revelation was given in addition to that written record.

The gift of prophecy may have been rather widely given in New Testament times, though the record mentions only a few prophets specifically. Prophets foretelling a famine came from Jerusalem to Antioch. One of these was named Agabus (Acts 11:27-28). Mention is made also of prophets in the church at Antioch (Acts 13:1), and Philip had four daughters who had the gift of prophecy (Acts 21:9). Prophets were also prominent in the Corinthian church (I Cor. 14).

C. Miracles (I Cor. 12:28) and Healing (I Cor. 12:9, 28, 30)

This is the ability to perform special signs. Paul exercised this gift at Ephesus when he performed miraculous healings (Acts 19:11-12). And yet, even though he had the gift of miracles, he did not consider it usable in the cases of Epaphroditus (Phil. 2:27) and Timothy (I Tim. 5:23). The gift of healing seems to be a specific category within the larger gift of miracles. An example of the gift of miracles which is not a case of physical healing was the blindness called down on Elymas the sorcerer in Paphos, Cyprus, by Paul on the first missionary journey (Acts 13:11).

Distinction should be made between miracles and healings and the gifts of miracles and healing. The spiritual gift is the God-given ability to perform miracles and healings for the purpose of serving Him. However, a miracle or a healing may be done apart from the exercise of the gifts. The miracle of the physical sign accompanying the filling with the Spirit recorded in Acts 4:31

was completely apart from the exercise of a gift on the part of any person. The miracle of Aeneas' healing at Lydda was apparently a result of Peter's exercising the gift of healing (Acts 9:34), while the raising of Dorcas at Joppa by Peter might not have been the result of exercising a gift but the result of God's answering prayer (Acts 9:40). Thus every miracle or every healing is not the result of the respective gift being exercised.

Consequently, then, it does not follow that if one considers the gifts of miracles and healings temporary, he also is saying that God does not perform miracles or heal today. He is simply saying that the gifts are no longer given because the particular purpose for which they were originally given (i.e., to authenticate the oral message) has ceased to exist. The historical proof for the cessation of the gift of miracles and the gift of healing with the accreditation of the message has been ably stated by B. B. Warfield in his book *Counterfeit Miracles*. The miracle of living epistles, he concludes, is the proper accreditation of the message of the gospel today.

If the giving of these particular gifts was limited to the early church, in what light is one to regard the question of healing today? Here are some issues to consider in finding the answer to that question.

1. As has been stated, God can and does heal apart from the exercise of the gift of healing. He does answer prayer, and He answers it in regard to physical problems; but such answers to prayer are not the exercise of the gift of healing.

2. It is obviously not the will of God to heal everybody. For example, it was not God's will to heal Paul of his thorn in the flesh (II Cor. 12:8-9).

3. Miracles and healing must not be equated with supernaturalism in general. It is a favorite pressure approach of faith healers to say that if you believe in the supernatural power of God, then you must also believe in His power to heal in the case at hand. This is simply not true, for it is a *non sequitur*. God does not have to use His supernatural power to prove that He possesses it. Furthermore, any gift given once has been given to the whole church.

4. To disregard human means in the matter of healing and simply pray for a miraculous cure is like praying for a harvest and then sitting in a rocking chair without planting or cultivat-

ing. God more often than not uses human means in the accomplishing of His purposes. This is true in matters of health too.

5. Those who claim that the gift of healing is exercised today have to admit that the gift is limited in its effectiveness, for they do not claim to heal decayed teeth or suddenly mend broken bones.

6. Reports of miraculous healings (within the limitations already stated) may be true (but this is not necessarily related to the gift), may be false, may be the cure of something that was psychosomatic.

Naturally all of these six considerations do not apply to every case, but they are germane to the whole question of healing today.

D. Tongues (I Cor. 12:10)

Tongues are the God-given ability to speak in another language. In the recorded instances in the book of Acts the languages of tongues seemed clearly to be foreign languages. There is no doubt that this was true at Pentecost, for the people heard in their native tongues; and it seemed to be the same kind of foreign languages that were spoken in the house of Cornelius (for Peter says that this was the same thing that occurred at Pentecost, Acts 10:46; 11:15).

The addition of the word "unknown" in I Corinthians 14 has led many to suppose that the tongues displayed in the church at Corinth were an unknown, heavenly language. If the word is omitted, then one would normally think of the tongues in Corinthians as the same as those in Acts; i.e., foreign languages. This is the natural conclusion. Against this view stand I Corinthians 14:2 and 14, which seem to indicate that the Corinthian tongues were an unknown language. In any case, the gift of tongues was being abused by the Corinthians, and Paul was required to lay down certain restrictions on its use. It was to be used only for edifying, only by two or three in a single meeting and then only if an interpreter were present, and never in preference to prophecy. The gift of interpretation is a corollary gift to the gift of tongues. The gift of tongues was given as a sign to unbelievers (I Cor. 14:22) and especially to unbelieving Jews (v. 21). If the need for the sign ceased, then of course the gift would no longer need to be given. (See section V on I Cor. 13:8.)

What about tongues today? One cannot say that God would never give this gift or other of the limited gifts today. But everything indicates that the need for the gift has ceased with the production of the written Word. Certainly the standard Pentecostal position that tongues are the necessary accompaniment of the baptism of the Holy Spirit is not valid (as has been discussed in Chapter 13). It is usually fruitless to discuss the experiences people have; one can only measure all experience by the written Word. Even if tongues be not a limited or temporary gift, the emphasis of Scripture is not on the use of this gift. Also, one should remember that the fruit of the Spirit does not include tongues, and Christlikeness does not require speaking in tongues, for Christ never did. At the same time, one agrees with René Pache who has wisely said: "May God give us humility and faithfulness enough to remain open to all that originates from Him and only to that."[1]

E. Evangelism (Eph. 4:11)

The meaning of the gift of evangelism involves two ideas—the kind of message preached (i.e., the good news of salvation) and the places where it is preached (i.e., in various places). The message is the gospel and the evangelist's ministry is an itinerant one. In the example of Paul's own life, the length of stay in one place on his itinerary sometimes lasted as long as two years (Acts 19:10) and sometimes only a few days (Acts 17:14). Apparently one may do the work of an evangelist even though he may not possess the gift, for Paul exhorts Timothy, who was a pastor, to do the work of an evangelist (II Tim. 4:5).

F. Pastor (Eph. 4:11)

The word "pastor" means to shepherd; therefore, the gift of pastor involves leading, providing and caring for, and protecting the portion of the flock of God committed to one's care. In Ephesians 4:11 the work of teaching is linked with that of pastoring, and in Acts 20:28 the duty of ruling the flock is added. The words "elder," "bishop," and "pastor" (translated "feed" in Acts 20:28) are all used of the same leaders of the Ephesian church (cf. Acts 20:17 and 28).

[1]*The Person and Work of the Holy Spirit* (Chicago: Moody Press, 1954), p. 195.

G. Ministering (Rom. 12:7; I Cor. 12:28; Eph. 4:12)

Ministering means serving. The gift of ministering is the gift of helping or serving in the broadest sense of the word. In the Romans passage it is called the gift of ministering; in I Corinthians, the gift of helps; in Ephesians we are told that other gifts are given for the purpose of helping believers to be able to serve. This is a very basic gift which all Christians can have and use for the Lord's glory.

H. Teaching (Rom. 12:7; I Cor. 12:28; Eph. 4:11)

Teaching is the God-given ability to explain the harmony and the detail of God's revelation. Apparently the gift is sometimes given alone (Rom. 12:7) and sometimes it is given along with the gift of pastor (Eph. 4:11). It is more obvious in the case of the gift of teaching that this is a gift that can be developed and must be trained. If we may assume that Peter had the gift, then it is clear that he had to do some studying of Paul's epistles before he could explain them to others (II Peter 3:16).

I. Faith (I Cor. 12:8-10)

Faith is the God-given ability to believe God's power to supply specific need. Every man has been given a measure of faith (Rom. 12:3), but not everyone has been given the gift of faith. Everyone may believe God, but this cannot be the same as possessing the gift of faith—otherwise there would be no significance to its being listed as a separate spiritual gift.

J. Exhortation (Rom. 12:8)

Exhorting involves encouraging, comforting, and admonishing people. Note that this is a separate and distinct gift from the gift of teaching. In other words, teaching may or may not involve exhortation, and contrariwise exhortation may or may not involve teaching.

K. Discerning Spirits (I Cor. 12:10)

Discerning spirits is the ability to distinguish between true and false sources of supernatural revelation when it was being given in oral form. It was a very necessary gift before the Word was written, for there were those who claimed to bring revelation from God who were not true prophets.

L. Showing Mercy (Rom. 12:8)

This is akin to the gift of ministering, for it involves succoring those who are sick and afflicted.

M. Giving (Rom. 12:8)

The gift of giving concerns distributing one's own money to others. It is to be done with simplicity; i.e., with no thought of return or gain for self in any way.

N. Administration (Rom. 12:8; I Cor. 12:28)

This is the ability to rule in the church.

V. I CORINTHIANS 13:8

Some consider that the expression "tongues shall cease" in I Corinthians 13:8 is a proof that tongues specifically was a limited gift. The argument against such an interpretation is that the passage is contrasting the present state with the eternal state and therefore is not speaking of the gift of tongues. However, it should be noted that the wider and immediate context is talking about the gift of tongues to a very great extent and there is no reason not to consider that it is the gift spoken of in this verse. It is also worthy of note that the principal thesis in Chapter 13 is that love never fails, even though tongues and prophecy do and even though the whole present imperfect state fails. There is no necessity in the passage to make the end of tongues the same time as the end of the imperfect or temporal state. Tongues could cease before time ceases and eternity begins without destroying the point of the passage. Indeed, such a progression may prove the point better; i.e., Paul is saying that (1) when tongues cease love abides, and (2) even when time itself comes to an end, love will abide.

There are positive indications in verse 8 that tongues would cease before prophecies and knowledge. Of prophecies (the oral communication of God's truth before the books of the canon were written) and knowledge (the special understanding of these prophecies) it is written that they shall be done away (*katargeo*, "rendered inoperative"). Of tongues it is said that they shall cease (*pauo*). Furthermore, the verb "done away" used in connection with prophecies and knowledge is in the passive voice, indicating that someone (God) shall make them inoperative.

The verb "cease" used in connection with tongues is middle voice, indicating that they would die out of their own accord.

Finally, it is rather significant that only prophecy and knowledge are mentioned in verse 9; tongues are not, as if Paul meant his readers to understand that the gift of tongues would cease before the gifts of prophecy and knowledge. After all, the fact that there are temporary gifts must have been quite evident in the early church (since the distinctiveness of apostles would have been very apparent to all). To indicate that tongues or other gifts were also temporary would have been no shock to the readers of the New Testament epistles. Unfortunately, we too easily forget today that the Scriptures clearly teach that some of the gifts were temporary (Eph. 2:20). It looks as if I Corinthians 13:8 specifies that the gift of tongues belongs to that category too.

16

THE FILLING OF THE SPIRIT

FROM THE VIEWPOINT of practice and experience the filling with the Spirit is the most important aspect of the doctrine of the Holy Spirit. It is the filling ministry that makes this doctrine experimental, so much of which is basically nonexperiential. Filling is the channel by which His ministries are worked in and through the believer. But, like many other aspects of the doctrine of the Holy Spirit it is not always clearly understood.

Spirit filling is necessary in order to experience the full extent of the ministry of the Spirit to a believer. In other words, it is necessary to growth in the spiritual life. All Christians belong in their spiritual experience and growth somewhere along the scale between immaturity and maturity. Maturity involves two things— time and continued control by the Holy Spirit. Thus a person may be immature either because he has not been a Christian very long or because, even though he has been a believer for a time, he has not been filled by the Spirit and therefore has not made any growth in the things of the Lord. The opposite of being controlled by the Spirit is being controlled by the flesh, or carnality. Carnality and spirituality are basically matters of control, although each kind of controlled life will, of course, exhibit distinct characteristics. But it is the control—not the characteristics— which makes one either carnal or spiritual.

I. THE CHARACTER OF BEING FILLED

A. Definition

The clue as to the proper definition of being filled with the Spirit is found in Ephesians 5:18: "And be not drunk with wine, wherein is excess; but be filled with the Spirit." While there is undoubtedly contrast in the verse between drunkenness and Spirit-filling, there is also comparison, and this furnishes the clue. The comparison is in the matter of control. A drunken person is controlled by the liquor which he has consumed. Because of this he thinks and acts in ways normally unnatural to him. Likewise, the man who is Spirit-filled is controlled, and he too acts in ways that are unnatural to him. This is not to imply that these ways are erratic or abnormal, but they are not ways which belong to his old life. Thus being filled with the Spirit is simply being controlled by the Spirit.

B. Demand

The Spirit-filled life is demanded in the Word. The verb in Ephesians 5:18 is an imperative. Christians are expected to be filled with the Spirit, and if such is not the case, then of course this is sin, for it is disobedience to a command of the Word.

C. Description

The most distinguishing feature of filling is that it is a repeated experience. This was not the case with baptism, indwelling, sealing, or regenerating, but it is the case with filling. This is proved by the present tense of the imperative in Ephesians 5:18 (which indicates continuous action), and it is illustrated in the life of the early church. The apostles were filled on the day of Pentecost (Acts 2:4). The same group was filled a short time later after the prayer meeting that came as a consequence of the Sanhedrin's questioning (Acts 4:31). That it can be repeated is a blessing, for it were not so, no believer would remain filled for long, since sin (which is ego-control) breaks the control of the Spirit.

II. THE CONDITIONS FOR BEING FILLED

Before leaving the earth the Lord commanded the disciples to tarry in Jerusalem for the fulfillment of the promise concerning the baptism of the Spirit. It is true that they were filled on the day of Pentecost, but this was not that for which they were tarrying. One searches in vain to find some example in the New Testament where believers are told to tarry or where they do tarry for the filling of the Spirit. Indeed, one searches without success to find an instance when believers ever prayed for the filling of the Spirit since the day of Pentecost. The nearest example of such a prayer is that of Paul's for the believers in Ephesus: "That the God of our Lord Jesus Christ, the Father of glory, may give unto you the spirit of wisdom and revelation in the knowledge of him" (Eph. 1:17). Yet this is not a prayer for the filling of the Spirit. There is no such example. But undoubtedly most people think this is the way to be Spirit-filled.

God does not ask believers either to tarry or to pray for the filling. This does not mean, however, that the filling is given without conditions. In a simple word the condition is obedience, and while prayer may be involved in meeting the demands of obedience, prayer (particularly seeking and tarrying prayer) will be of no avail in obtaining the filling. Obedience is the condition, and the Scripture explains what is meant by obedience in detailed terms as it relates to the filling of the Spirit.

A. A Dedicated Life

Of all the outlines on the conditions for the filling of the Spirit, none is more simple, scriptural, and to the point than Lewis Sperry Chafer's in *He That Is Spiritual*. It is this outline that we follow in detailing what is meant by obedience as the condition for being filled with the Holy Spirit.

In order to be Spirit-filled there must first be dedication of life. This, Chafer suggests, is epitomized in the text of I Thessalonians 5:19: "Quench not the Spirit." Exegetically and contextually the verse primarily has to do with quenching prophesyings in the public assembly of the church. The word quench is used of putting out a fire (Mark 9:48; Heb. 11:34) and is used appropriately in relation to the Spirit (cf. Matt. 3:11; Acts 2:3). The verb is in the present imperative and thus means "stop quenching the Spirit"; that is, stop doing something you are now doing. The church in Thessalonica was frowning on any manifestation of the Spirit that was in any way out of the ordinary. (Contrast the situation in Corinth where Paul had to warn the church against an overmanifestation and disorderliness in relation to gifts of the Spirit.)

Though this is the meaning exegetically, Chafer has taken the verse to stand for the theological truth that dedication is foundational to Spirit-filling. Such dedication concerns the basic policy of one's relation to the will of God *in toto* and not especially to specifics within the will of God.

1. The method of a dedicated life. A dedicated life involves two things—initial dedication and continued dedication through constant direction of that life.

a. Initial dedication (Rom. 12:1-2). Initial dedication is a crisis and a once-for-all matter. According to the central passage, Romans 12:1-2, it involves three things.

First there must be a presentation. The tense is aorist (which indicates an unrepeated event), and the object is the body. Thus this dedication is a crisis and complete thing. It is not a succession of acts, and it involves the entire life of the believer. Although initial dedication may be brought about by some particular problem or decision, it is not a dedication to do something but a dedication of the entire life, which of course involves everything. Basically the question is: Who will run the life—Christ or self? This is certainly not snipping off one sin at a time. It is a complete offering of self once and for all. Neither does it merely involve the lacks in one's life; it means the offering of the good talents as well.

Second, it involves a separation (v. 2). The tense is present and the mood imperative which means "stop being conformed to this world." The word is very vivid. It means: Do not appear veneered with the world when you are a Christian underneath. It is the picture of a cheap finish on top of an expensive base.

Third, it involves a transformation that is continual. This transformation centers in the mind, for there is controlled all the thought patterns of life, and such transformation will result in a knowledge of the will of God. Basic to all this, however, is the initial act of presentation or dedication. This must take place first; otherwise there can be no separation or transformation.

b. Continual direction. The dedicated life needs direction, for dedication does not automatically guarantee the solution to all life's problems. It does guarantee (or should) that when faced with a problem the Christian will need only to discern the will of God, not to debate whether or not he will do it. But in order to know what God's will is in particular circumstances, it is necessary to have direction from the Holy Spirit, and then to follow that direction in order to be Spirit-filled. It is the Spirit who leads (Rom. 8:14), and He does it basically through fellowship with Himself, which presupposes the yieldedness of initial dedication. Thus dedication is kept active and pertinent by daily direction of the Spirit as the believer walks in fellowship with Him.

Suggestions as to how to discern the leading of the Spirit are legion. Fellowship so intimate that there can be no doubt as to His leading is the key to the matter. However, some additional suggestions may be in order.

(1) Substitutes should not be sought for fellowship. The fleece in order to determine the Lord's leading limits God to two possibilities. The fleece after a decision has been made in order to confirm the Lord's leading is quite a different thing. The lot likewise limits God to as many ways as can be thought of. But, of course, He may have a different way in mind which has not been thought of.

(2) A knowledge of the Word of God is essential. God never leads in a manner contrary to the Word; indeed, He leads on the basis of the Word. The Word tells one both how God will not lead and how He will lead.

(3) Friends are valuable in giving information and counsel. The wisdom of older Christians is invaluable. But ultimately the leading is up to the individual believer, not to or through his friends.

(4) Care should be exercised in trying to have the same prescription filled twice. Above all, a friend's prescription should never be used as to one's leading. It might be poison to another person.

(5) The whole matter should be talked over with the Lord. He will not only show the answer but also the way to recognize the answer. All doubts and problems and fears should be told to Him; then one should wait until He makes the way clear. Knowing when to wait is just as definite a leading as knowing when to move.

2. The manifestations of a dedicated life. A directed life is a life of peace, for it is a life lived in the will of God. A directed life is not a sinless life, but it is a life lived in the right path and one that grows and matures day by day. Dedication of life, including the basic initial act of dedication and the continuous life of direction by the Spirit, is the first prerequisite for the Spirit-filled life.

B. An Undefeated Life

The day-by-day problem of sin in the life must be recognized and be dealt with if the Spirit is to control that life. Dedication and direction are factors but victory over sin in daily experience is another matter.

As a text to summarize this concept Chafer used Ephesians 4:30: "And grieve not the holy Spirit of God, whereby ye are sealed unto the day of redemption." Exegetically the verse does concern the effect of certain sins in the person's relation to the Spirit. He is grieved by sin, but He does not remove His presence from that life. Those certain sins in the context of Ephesians 4:30 are sins of speech. Useless speech (v. 29), bitterness, wrath, anger, clamor, and evil speaking (v. 31) are mentioned. In the following verses other forms of unbecoming speech are listed (5:4). Thus it is clear that sins of speech are those which particularly grieve the Spirit so that His ministry in the believer's life is hindered. Theologically we may permit the verse to represent and remind of any sin which grieves the Spirit. The matter of an undefeated-by-sin life is vital, then, to the control or filling by the Spirit, for when He is grieved by sin He is not in control.

1. God's purpose concerning sin in the life. God's purpose concerning sin in the believer's life involves three factors.

a. It involves godliness. God's own holiness is the standard by which all sin is measured. This is expressed in a number of verses. "For all have sinned, and come short of the glory of God" (Rom. 3:23). "But as he which hath called you is holy, so be ye holy in all manner of conversation, because it is written, Be ye holy; for I am holy" (I Peter 1:15-16). "This then is the message which we have heard of him, and declare unto you, that God is light, and in him is no darkness at all" (I John 1:5). God, who is light, is Himself the standard. Of course, no one can meet that perfect standard, so God, without lowering the standard, has wisely tailored it to each individual Christian so that he can meet his own requirement. God has done this by requiring that we walk in the light. In other words, we are required to respond to all the light which we as growing Christians receive. He is the standard; He constantly and increasingly reveals Himself; He expects us to respond continually to that ever-growing revelation of Himself. This is what it means to walk in the light. Lack of response in any particular is sin and grieves the Spirit so that He does not fully control the life.

b. It involves genuineness. One of the secrets of spiritual victory is openness before the Lord. It is obvious that He does know even the secrets of the heart, but a realization of that will make one's response to the light as keen as it should be.

c. It involves grace. Grace is necessary in this walk simply because we do fail. But when we fail He does not cast us off; He forgives when we confess our sins (I John 1:9). If it were not for His grace, we would all have been lost long ago.

2. God's provision concerning sin in the life. God's provision concerning sin is threefold.

a. Crucifixion. Reckoning true the co-crucifixion of the sin nature with Christ in His death unto sin is the basic provision for victory (Rom. 6:1-13). In a sense this is similar to the initial dedication of life in that it is a crisis experience, but in another very vital sense it is different in that it is not a presentation but a reckoning true of that which is already accomplished. Without this there can be no victory over habitual sin in the life.

b. Chastisement. God's discipline is also His provision concerning sin in the believer's life (Heb. 12:5-11). The express purpose of such chastening is "for our profit, that we might be partakers of his holiness" (v. 10).

c. Confession and cleansing. But sin we will as long as we are in these bodies. Therefore God has made provision for restoring fellowship by our confessing (I John 1:9). To confess means to agree, and in this verse it means to agree with God concerning the particular sin; that is, we must have God's viewpoint on the sin. It is not merely rehearsing the sin before God but admitting that what He thinks about the sin is actually how bad it is. When this is done, then He faithfully and righteously forgives and restores to full fellowship or enjoyment of the salvation which was, of course, never lost by the sin.

The victorious life or the life which does not grieve the Holy Spirit is the undefeated life. It is the life which is constantly responding to the light as it is revealed in God's Word. As response is made, this will bring to light more areas of darkness which then need to be confessed. Then more light comes, which in turn requires more confession of newly discovered darkness. And so it goes throughout life, but this is the normally developing life which grieves not the Spirit.

C. A Dependent Life

Finally, the Spirit-filled life is a dependent life. "This I say then, Walk in the Spirit, and ye shall not fulfill the lust of the flesh" (Gal. 5:16).

1. The nature of it. By its very nature, walking is a succession of dependent acts. When one foot is lifted in order to place it in front of the other one, it is done so in faith that the foot remaining on the ground will support the full weight of the body. Each foot in turn acts as a support while the other foot is being moved forward. One can only make progress by walking by faith in relation to the one foot and dependence on the other. In this verse in Galatians the Christian is reminded that in order to walk and make progress in the Christian life he must walk by faith, which means to live in dependence on the Holy Spirit. "Walk *by* the Spirit" is the correct translation.[1]

2. The need for it. This continual walk of dependence is required by the following considerations.

a. Because the standards are high. The requirements of grace are the highest of standards. The love demanded is the love of Christ (John 13:34). It can be shed abroad in a life only by the full unhindered ministry of the Spirit (Rom. 5:5). Every thought is required to be brought into obedience (II Cor. 10:5). "In everything give thanks" (I Thess. 5:18). "Pray without ceasing" (I Thess. 5:17). These are all standards which require dependence on the Spirit if they are ever to be met.

b. Because the enemies are powerful. The dependent life is necessary because the enemies are strong. The devil stalks as a roaring lion, seeking to devour utterly the believer's testimony (I Peter 5:8). Even friendship with the world sets one at enmity with God (James 4:4). In the flesh dwells no good thing (Rom. 7:18), and this very weakness promotes the power of the sin nature.

Only by walking in dependence on the Spirit—that is, letting

---

[1]"*Pneumati*, the *normal* dative, of the rule, or manner, after or in which: . . . —by the Spirit. But *pn.* is not man's '*spiritual part*,' . . . nor is *pneumati* '*after a spiritual manner*,' . . . it is (as in v. 5) the Holy Spirit of God: this will be clear on comparing with our vv. 16-18, the more expanded parallel passage, Rom. vii.22-viii.11. The history of the verbal usage is, that *pneuma*, as *christos* and *theos*, came to be used as a proper name: so that the supposed distinction between *to pn.* as the objective (the Holy Ghost), and *pn.* as the subjective (man's spirit), does not hold" (*Alford's Greek Testament*, III, 57).

the Spirit have full control—can the Christian ever hope to make the progress that is consonant with his profession.

Thus to be Spirit-filled is to be Spirit-controlled. And to be so controlled requires dedication of life, victory over the reigning power of sin, and constant dependence on the Spirit. These are the conditions for Spirit-control. Prayer and human effort may be involved in order to meet the conditions, but when they are met, the Spirit's control automatically follows. One's attention ought not to be on praying to be filled; rather it ought to be on being sensitive to these conditions; for when they are being met, the filling will be experienced.

III. THE CONSEQUENCES OF BEING FILLED

Being Spirit-filled results in the experiential realization of all the ministries of the Spirit. For instance, though a believer is sealed, regenerated, baptized, and indwelt whether he realizes it or not, he will come to realize these facts and enjoy the benefits of them when he is filled with the Spirit. In addition to this, however, certain other ministries of the Spirit are linked in the Scriptures with filling. These may properly be classed as direct consequences of being filled or controlled by the Spirit.

A. A Christlike Character (Gal. 5:22-23)

The fruit of the Spirit is inseparably linked with the filling of the Spirit in Galatians 5. Paul contrasts in this chapter the works of the flesh and the fruit of the Spirit. He declares that the means of not fulfilling the lusts of the flesh is to walk in dependence on the Spirit—a condition for the filling (v. 16). Then he pictures in vivid detail the lusts of the flesh (vv. 19-21) and sets in contrast to them the fruit of the Spirit (vv. 22-23). It has often been pointed out that this fruit produced by being filled by the Spirit is a perfect picture of Christlikeness. And so it is. Therefore, it may be said that one of the consequences of being Spirit-filled is the producing of Christlikeness.

This involves, as far as this passage is concerned, nine features. The first is love, which is seeking the glory of God in the object loved. There may be acts which on the surface appear to be unkind but which are in reality an expression of love, if the goal is the glory of God. Love and knowledge are vitally related, for the deepest kind of love is based on the fullest knowledge. Joy is primarily derived from seeing other Christians advance in the knowledge of the truth (III John 4). Peace is that tranquillity which comes because one is rightly related to God. Long-suffering is the evenness of character and action which never displays a desire for revenge. Gentleness is beneficent thoughts, while goodness is kind actions. Faithfulness means serving with regularity and buying up all the opportunities with every faculty given to us by God. Meekness is gentlemanliness and in no way includes the concept of weakness. Self-control is discipline of the whole life, including especially areas of morality.

This is the fruit of the Spirit, and this Christlike character is produced only by the Spirit completely controlling or filling the life.

B. Worship and Praise (Eph. 5:18-20)

The classic verse on the filling of the Spirit (Eph. 5:18) is followed immediately in its context by at least four consequences of being filled. The first is the outward expression of praise through "speaking to one another [note correct translation] in psalms and hymns and spiritual songs." The second is the inner expression of praise by "singing and making melody in your heart to the Lord." The third consequence of being controlled by the Spirit is a thankful heart.

C. Submissiveness (Eph. 5:21)

Another consequence of being Spirit-filled is a submission to one another that will affect all the relationships of life, so that peace and harmony will reign between husbands and wives, parents and children, employers and employees. Control by self will mean an expression of self which will disrupt the harmony that ought to exist in all relationships of life.

D. Service (John 7:37-39)

It was the eighth day of the Feast of Tabernacles when these words were spoken. "The image appears to have been occasioned by the libations of water brought in a golden vessel from Siloam which were made at the time of the morning sacrifice on each of the seven days of the feast while Isa. xii. 3 was sung. It is uncertain whether the libations were made on the eighth day. If they were not made, the significant cessation of the striking rite on this one day of the feast would give a still more fitting occasion for the words."[2]

When Christ is received, not only is the soul's own thirst satisfied but the blessing received becomes the blessing distributed. The believer not only satisfies himself but he overflows in service to others. This overflowing is the ministry of the Spirit through a controlled life, and it is a ministry distinctive to this age according to the Lord's words.

The full realization of other ministries of the Spirit depends on being filled with the Spirit. However, these three in a particular way seem to depend more completely on the filling. Filling means control—100 percent control of all known matters and areas of the Christian's life. Such control is prerequisite to Christlikeness, praise, and service. Other ministries of the Spirit, such as teaching, will never be fully realized by the believer unless he is consciously controlled by the Spirit, but to a certain extent they might be experienced even by the one who is not filled. Therefore, these other ministries, though they are in a certain sense consequences of filling, will be considered in the next chapter.

[2]B. F. Westcott, *The Gospel According to St. John* (London: J. Murray), I, 277.

17

OTHER MINISTRIES OF THE SPIRIT

I. TEACHING

THE TEACHING MINISTRY of the Spirit was one of the last promises of the Saviour before His crucifixion. In the upper room He said, "I have yet many things to say unto you, but ye cannot bear them now. Howbeit when he, the Spirit of truth, is come, he will guide you into all truth: for he shall not speak of himself; but whatsoever he shall hear, that shall he speak: and he will show you things to come. He shall glorify me: for he shall receive of mine, and shall show it unto you. All things that the Father hath are mine: therefore said I, that he shall take of mine, and shall show it unto you" (John 16:12-15).

A. Time

This particular ministry of the Spirit was yet future when our Lord spoke these words. It was begun on the day of Pentecost and continues throughout this age. Peter's clear comprehension as revealed in his Pentecostal sermon is evidence of the beginning of this ministry.

B. Content

In general the content of the Spirit's ministry encompasses "all the truth" (the definite article appears in the Greek text). This, of course, means revelation concerning Christ Himself, but on the basis of the written Word (for we have no other information about Him except through the Bible). Therefore, He teaches the believer the content of the Scripture which leads him to an understanding of prophecy ("things to come"). This particularizing of the general promise concerning teaching ought to encourage every believer to study prophecy. Notice, too, that the Spirit does not originate His message—it comes from the Lord.

C. Result

The result of the teaching ministry of the Spirit is that Christ is glorified. If He is not glorified, then the Spirit has not been ministering. Note also that it is not the Spirit who is glorified or who is supposed to be glorified in a religious service, but Christ. Further, if Christ is known only through the written Word, then He will be glorified when the Word of God is expounded in the power of the Spirit.

D. Procedure

How does the Spirit teach the believer? John flatly declares: "But the anointing which ye have received of him abideth in you, and ye need not that any man teach you: but as the same anointing teacheth you of all things, and is truth, and is no lie, and even as it hath taught you, ye shall abide in him" (I John 2:27). This could not mean that human teachers are unnecessary in explaining the Word of God. If it could, then what would be the use of the gift of teaching (Rom. 12:7)? John wrote concerning the presence of antichrists in the group. Having stated his own conviction concerning their heresies, he simply declared that no man really had to tell them the truth, for the Holy Spirit would confirm it to them. Human teachers are a necessary link in the procedure of instructing believers, though the ultimate authentication of the teaching comes from the Spirit.

II. GUIDING

"For as many as are led by the Spirit of God, they are the sons of God" (Rom. 8:14). Leading is a confirmation of sonship, for sons are led. Much has already been said (in Chapter 16) about guidance in connection with dedication. This work of guidance is particularly the work of the Spirit. Romans 8:14 states it and the book of Acts amply illustrates it (Acts 8:29; 10:19-20; 13:2, 4; 16:6-7; 20:22-23). The various means the Spirit may use have already been discussed in the previously cited section. This ministry of the Spirit is one of the most blessedly assuring ones for the Christian. The child of God need never be walking in the dark; he is always free to ask and receive directions from the Spirit Himself.

III. ASSURING

The Spirit is also the one who assures the Christian that he is a child of God. "The Spirit itself [himself] beareth witness with our spirit, that we are the children of God" (Rom. 8:16). The Greek word for children here is *tekna* (in contrast to *huioi*, sons) and emphasizes the fact that the believer shares in the life of the Father. Because of this, he also shares as an heir in the possessions of the Father. Assurance of all this is the work of the Spirit to the heart of each Christian.

Undoubtedly assurance is also brought to the heart of the believer by an increased understanding of some of the things which the Spirit has done for him. For instance, assurance will deepen when one understands what it means to be sealed with the Spirit and to have been given the earnest of the Spirit as a guarantee of the completion of redemption (Eph. 1:13-14). The comprehension of what is involved in the Spirit's joining the believer to the risen, undying body of Christ will also nurture assurance. Of course, the comprehension of these great accomplishments is part of the teaching ministry of the Spirit, so in many ways the Holy Spirit is connected with and concerned about the assurance of the child of God.

IV. PRAYING

A. The Statement

Although we may not fully understand the ramifications of the Spirit's praying in the believer, the fact that He does is perfectly clear: "Likewise the Spirit also helpeth our infirmities: for we know not what we should pray for as we ought: but the Spirit itself [himself] maketh intercession for us with groanings which cannot be uttered" (Rom. 8:26).

B. The Need

The stated reason why we need help is because of our infirmity (the word is singular). He helps our entire weakness but especially as it manifests itself in relation to our prayer life, and particularly in relation to knowing what to pray for at the present moment. While we wait for our full redemption we need guidance in the particulars of prayer.

C. The Method

The way the Spirit helps meet our need is described in general by the word "helpeth," which literally means "puts His hand to the work in cooperation with us."[1] Specifically this help is given in the form of "groanings which cannot be uttered." These groanings, the meaning of which cannot be grasped, find no adequate or formulated expression. One thing we do know—they are according to the will of God.

In another passage we are told that the Spirit guides and directs our prayers (Eph. 6:18). This is more the guidance of the believer's heart and mind as he prays than the unutterable groanings of the Spirit Himself.

D. The Result

The result of such a prayer life is assurance to the believer of the certainty of his future and full redemption (Rom. 8:23). This ministry of the Spirit is a kind of earnestlike guarantee of that redemption. Such a satisfying prayer life will help keep us content in this present world as we wait for the consummation. The ministry of the Spirit, then, is not only connected with answered prayer, but it cultivates our assurance and contentment in this life.

[1]R. St. John Parry, *Romans, Cambridge Greek Testament* (New York: Cambridge University Press, 1912), p. 120.

18

THE ESCHATOLOGY OF THE HOLY SPIRIT

I. THE SPIRIT IN THE TRIBULATION PERIOD

IN THE OPINION of the writer, the Church will be removed from the earth before the tribulation begins. Involved in this pretribulational rapture concept is the removal of the restrainer at the same time (II Thess. 2:6-8). That is, the guaranteed indwelling presence of the Spirit in believers will necessitate the removal of the Spirit when believers are raptured. However, such removal does not mean or even imply that the work of the Spirit comes to an end. Just as the omnipresent Spirit worked in behalf of men in Old Testament times, so He will continue to work after the rapture of the Church, even though His work of building the Body of Christ will be finished.

A. In Relation to Unbelievers

During the tribulation period multitudes of people will be converted. (1) At the beginning of the period God will seal 144,000 Jews, and this sealing involves their salvation (Rev. 7:4; 14:4). (2) During the tribulation a multitude which is so large that it cannot be numbered will turn to the Lord from "all nations, and kindreds, and people, and tongues" (Rev. 7:9). This group is said specifically to come out of the great tribulation (Rev. 7:14). (3) At the end of the time those Israelites who are living and who pass successfully through the judgment will be converted (Rom. 11:25; Zech. 13:1). In this latter case the work of the Spirit is connected with the salvation of unsaved people in the tribulation period (Zech. 12:10). In the other instances there is no specific reference to the part the Spirit may have in conversion, though it would not seem out of place to assume that He will have a part.

108

B. In Relation to Believers

Apparently the Spirit's work in believers during the tribulation period will follow the pattern of His work in the Old Testament. He will be present and active in the world; He will indwell and empower His people; He will use believers in witnessing. Specific proof texts are scarce, for the Bible says very little about the Spirit's ministry during that time. One text that can be used is the quotation of Joel 2 in Acts 2, because for whatever purpose it was quoted on the day of Pentecost, it obviously did not have a complete fulfillment on that day. Full fulfillment awaits the tribulation days, since the passage expressly links the pouring out of the Spirit with the time when the sun will be turned to darkness and the moon to blood. These events will occur at the close of the tribulation just before the second coming of Christ (Matt. 24:29-30). Another possible proof text is Revelation 11:3-4, which links the ministry of the two witnesses during the tribulation to the power of the Spirit (Zech. 4:6).

C. In Relation to Other Ministries of the Spirit

While it seems that there will be a widespread ministry of the Spirit during this time, His ministry of baptizing believers into the Body of Christ will not occur then. The reason is simple: There will be no purpose for the baptism since the Body of Christ will be complete before the period begins. Too, His work of restraining by means of indwelling believers as the temple of God will not carry over into the tribulation. However, this does not mean that He may not restrain during that time, for He did restrain in days before the Body of Christ came into existence (Gen. 6:3).

II. THE SPIRIT IN THE MILLENNIUM

A. In Relation to Unbelievers

When the millennium begins, it appears that at that moment all who are a part of it will be redeemed. Living Jews will have been judged and the rebels from among them purged out (Ezek. 20:33-44; Zech. 13:8-9). Living Gentiles, too, will fall under the judgment of God (Matt. 25:31-46). As a result of these two judgments, all who enter the millennium will be redeemed. However, children will be born throughout the millennium, with the result that during that time many will be in need of salvation and many will receive it. This work of salvation is related to the Spirit in the case of Israel and the fulfillment of her new covenant (Jer. 31:31-34; Ezek. 36:25-31; Zech. 12:10; 14:16).

B. In Relation to Believers

The new covenant also provides for the indwelling of the Spirit in believing Israel during the millennial age (Jer. 31:33). This relationship of the Spirit apparently also includes His filling as well as indwelling (Joel 2:28-29).

C. In Relation to Christ

During the millennium the fullness of the Spirit on Christ will be evident (Isa. 11:2-3). The period will be the fullest display of the presence and power of God that the earth has ever seen since the days of Adam and, although little is said specifically concerning the Spirit's work, His ministry along with the other persons of the Trinity will be abundantly manifest. Yet in spite of all that God will do for man in those years, Satan will find a ready response in the hearts of many who will side with him in his final and futile revolt against Messiah (Rev. 20:7-9). This serves as final proof of the wickedness of man's heart and of his need of the regenerating work of the Holy Spirit.

19

HISTORY OF THE DOCTRINE OF THE SPIRIT

I. TO THE COUNCIL OF NICEA

A. Orthodox Witness

Doctrinal formulation of the Christian faith did not occur all at once at some point in the history of the church. Nor did a definition of all Christian doctrines take place at any equal rate. Sometimes one doctrine came in for attention; at other times the spotlight would focus on a different doctrine.

The doctrine of the Holy Spirit did not receive much attention in the early centuries as far as formal definition was concerned. What we have come to know as the orthodox expression of the doctrine of the Spirit was witnessed to by the early church in the baptismal formula, in the Apostles' Creed, and in the castigating of error when it did appear. The use of the threefold name of Father, Son, and Spirit shows that implicitly and in practice the deity and personality of the Spirit were acknowledged by the early church.

As far as the Spirit was concerned, the principal emphasis in the subapostolic age was on the experience of the Spirit rather than the doctrine. This emphasis is particularly notable in *The Shepherd of Hermas*. In the era of the apologists the Spirit is very much in the background of the literature, since the emphasis was on the Logos. At the same time there seemed to be no erroneous experience of the Spirit in spite of the lack of doctrinal definition.

B. Montanism (150)

It was in Montanism that the subject of the Holy Spirit came into more prominence. The original impetus for this movement grew out of a reaction against the increasing rigidity and frigidity of the organized church. Montanism (also called the Phrygian heresy) appeared in Phrygia about 150 through the ministry

111

of Montanus and two women, Prisca and Maximilla. They announced themselves as prophets and announced the period as the age of the Paraclete in which new revelations from God were to be given. They emphasized the nearness of the end of the world and insisted on very high and strict moral standards in their followers. It was this high morality which attracted Tertullian and others to the movement.

It should be remembered that Montanism was an orthodox movement in contrast to gnosticism. It was also a reaction against gnosticism with its intellectualism, which seemingly raised a barrier against the soul's personal communication with God. For many, Montanism stood for the active presence and ministry of the Spirit in the church and for a more spiritual type of church life. However, Montanism was officially rejected because of its insistence on additional revelation, and in so doing, the church affirmed the belief that the Spirit does not give new revelations apart from the Scriptures. Still with all this emphasis on the experience of the Spirit the doctrine remained for the most part without formulation.

C. Sabellianism (215)

Monarchianism was the predecessor of Sabellianism. In its modalistic form, Monarchianism taught that the Son was merely a mode of expression of the Father. Noetus and Praxeas were leaders in this movement, and they also taught patripassianism (i.e., the Father was crucified). Since the Monarchians taught that the Son was a mode of expression of God, it was inevitable that the church was forced to consider the relation of the Spirit to the Son and to the Father. Sabellius taught that God is a unity but that He revealed Himself in three different modes or forms. These three forms were not three hypostases but three roles or parts played by the one God. Sabellianism was the first major error concerning the Trinity which gained a large following in the church.

D. Arianism (325)

The Arian controversy is thus called because it was occasioned by the anti-Trinitarian views of Arius, a presbyter of Alexandria. The monotheistic principle of Monarchianism was a dominant concept in his view. However, he distinguished the one eternal

God from the Son who was generated by the Father and who had a beginning. He also believed that the Holy Spirit was the first thing created by the Son, for all things were made by the Son. Arius was opposed by Athanasius, and the Council of Nicea was called to discuss the dispute.

The principal statement of the council concerned the deity of the Second Person, and the conclusion was that Christ was "of the same substance" as the Father. The attention of the council was focused on the Son rather than the Spirit, and the Nicene Creed merely mentions the Spirit: "I believe in the Holy Spirit." The statement can be said only to infer the deity and personality of the Holy Spirit because of its connection with the specific declaration concerning the Son. Why the council was not equally specific concerning the Spirit is only a matter of conjecture. Possibly the church was content not to anticipate heresy or to go beyond what the occasion demanded. Athanasius, however, was much more definite in his own teaching, vigorously maintaining that the Spirit, like the Son, was of the same essence as the Father.

II. FROM NICEA TO THE PROTESTANT REFORMATION

A. The Council of Constantinople (381)

All was not settled by the Nicene Council. Although Athanasius' own teaching was clearly orthodox and detailed, the Nicene Creed had been indefinite concerning the Spirit. A new controversy soon arose and people began to assert their unbelief in the deity of the Spirit. As a result, there arose the Macedonians, whose founder, Macedonius, bishop of Constantinople, maintained that the Spirit was a creature subordinate to the Son. His party was nicknamed Pneumatomachians ("evil speakers against the Spirit"). The main stream of orthodox teaching was that the Holy Spirit was divine or else the Son was not divine. Basil of Caesarea, Gregory of Nazianzus, and Gregory of Nyssa were leaders in propagating the orthodox view and preparing the way for the Council of Constantinople.

The controversy grew to such proportions that Emperor Theodosius had to call a council at Constantinople consisting of 150 orthodox bishops representing the Eastern church only. In 381 the council met and under the guidance of Gregory of Nazianzus formulated the following statement concerning the Holy Spirit: "And we believe in the Holy Spirit, the Lord, the Life-giving, who proceeds from the Father, who is to be glorified with the Father and the Son, and who speaks through the prophets." It has been pointed out that the creed used remarkable moderation in avoiding the term "of the same substance" (which was used of Christ in the Nicene Creed) to express the Spirit's oneness with the Father and the Son. Actually the Spirit is not even called God in the creed, though the terms in which His work is described cannot possibly be predicated of any created being. Nevertheless, the statement did counter the Macedonians, even though it did not assert the consubstantiality of the Spirit with the Father or define the relation of the Spirit to the Father and the Son; and it settled the question of the deity of the Spirit just as the Nicene Council had settled the question of the deity of⸱Christ.

B. Augustine (354-430)

1. *De Trinitate.* The concept of the Trinity in the Western church reached a final formulation in this work by Augustine. His interest in the doctrine of grace would naturally lead to a consideration of the Spirit, for his own experiences taught him how necessary the power of the Spirit is to the believer. In this treatise he stated that each of the three persons of the Trinity possesses the entire essence and that all are interdependent on the others. He declared that he was not satisfied with the word "persons" to express the three hypostases, but he used it "in order not to be silent." In his conception of the Trinity, the Spirit proceeds from both the Father and the Son.

2. The Pelagian controversy (431). Augustine also laid great stress on efficacious grace as the work of the Spirit. This profoundly influenced not only his doctrine of man and of sin but also his doctrine of the Spirit. Pelagius, his opponent in the controversy, advocated a practical denial of original sin and emphasized the ability of man to do good apart from the enablement of the Spirit. The Council of Ephesus dealt with the controversy in 431 and condemned Pelagius and his views and upheld Augustine and his. Although Pelagianism was condemned officially, it was not eradicated from the church, for Pelagianism and semi-

Pelagianism (as well as Augustinianism) have come down to this present day.

C. The Council of Chalcedon (451)

In 451 the Council of Chalcedon, representing the sees of Rome, Constantinople, Antioch, and Jerusalem, confirmed the decisions of Nicea and Constantinople. The council explicitly stated that the Nicene Creed was sufficient as a proper statement of the doctrine of the Trinity and that the clauses added by the Council of Constantinople in 381 were only intended to clarify, not change the Nicene Creed. This firmly established the doctrine of the deity of the Holy Spirit.

D. The Synod of Toledo (589)

Although the question of the deity of the Spirit had been settled at Constantinople and Chalcedon, there still remained the important and mysterious question of the Spirit's precise relation to the Father and the Son. This was a problem that developed in the West (the matter of the deity of the Spirit was Eastern). The term "generation" was used to describe the relation of the Son to the Father, while the term "procession" was employed to denote the relation of the Spirit. The question was: Did the Spirit proceed from the Father only, or from the Father and the Son? Although the Council of Constantinople did not declare that the Spirit proceeded from the Son as well as from the Father, this was the belief of many church leaders. It was felt necessary to believe that, lest procession from the Father only look like a denial of the essential oneness of the Son with the Father. However, there was not unanimity on this point, for others felt that to say that the Spirit proceeded from the Father and the Son would mean that the Spirit was dependent on the Son and would thus infringe on His deity.

The Western theologians held to the procession from the Father and the Son, and they added the famous "filioque" ("and Son") clause to the Constantinopolitan Creed at the Synod of Toledo. The clause stated that the Spirit "proceedeth from the Father and the Son." How the "filioque" clause came into the creed is a matter of discussion. Some think it was the "blunder" of a copyist. In any case, the clause never caused suspicion but was repeated synod after synod as orthodox doctrine. Leaders in the Eastern church felt that the Western church was tampering with the creed set at Constantinople and never adopted the "filioque" addition, declaring it heresy to this day.

Thus three things concerning the Trinity were settled beyond all question, at least in the Western church. The deity of the Son was settled at the Council of Nicea; the deity of the Spirit at Constantinople; and the procession of the Spirit from the Father and the Son at the Synod of Toledo. The presence of heresy had forced the church to settle these great doctrinal matters.

E. Abelard (1079-1142)

Abelard spoke of the Trinity in ways which caused him to be charged with Sabellianism. The name of the Father, he said, stands for power; the Son, for wisdom; the Spirit, for goodness. Sometimes he seemed to indicate real personal distinctions in the Godhead, but his illustrations and expressions at other times were modalistic.

F. Thomas Aquinas (1227-1274)

In Thomas there was the usual orthodox understanding of the Trinity. Generally speaking, however, the centuries preceding the Protestant Reformation added little to the doctrine of the Spirit beyond what was so well systematized by Augustine. In the West, while the influence of Augustine was still at work, the church became semi-Pelagian (de-emphasizing original sin and emphasizing the freedom of man's will). This together with the increasing sacerdotalism and its consequences (which promoted special powers of the clergy) tended to keep the minds of many away from any further study of the Holy Spirit. Although there were tendencies toward mysticism on the part of some, no real fresh study of the doctrine of the Spirit was made until the time of the Reformation.

III. FROM THE REFORMATION TO THE PRESENT

A. The Protestant Reformation (1517)

Up to the time of the Reformation the church's attention had been directed only toward the person of the Spirit. In the Reformation attention was given to His work. As far as the Spirit's person was concerned, all the Reformed confessions express the orthodox doctrine of the Spirit in relation to the other persons of the Trinity. As far as His work is concerned, there was renewed emphasis on the necessity of His work in regenerating man because there was a return to the Augustinian emphasis on the total depravity of man.

Another important contribution of the Reformers was their emphasis on the need of illumination by the Spirit. The Roman church taught that only the priest could interpret the Word of God, while the Reformers advocated openly the study of the Bible, asserting that all believers could be taught its truths by the teaching ministry of the Holy Spirit.

Luther's emphasis on justification by faith caused him to say much about the Spirit's work in this connection. Calvin emphasized those aspects of the work of the Spirit which are associated with the Trinity and the ministry of the Spirit in the hearts and lives of believers.

The various documents and creeds growing out of the Reformation are uniform in their orthodoxy. The Augsburg Confession, the Anglican Articles, the Formula Concordiae, the Helvetic Confession, and the Westminster Confession all asserted the deity of the Spirit following the Council of Chalcedon, including the "filioque" clause as well as the particular emphases brought to light by the Reformation itself. Indeed, it may be said that it was not until the time of the Reformation that there was a developed doctrine of the Holy Spirit.

B. The Socinians and Arminians

Almost every religious movement is followed by excesses and reactions. The Reformation was no exception. Some went to an extreme of unbalanced enthusiasm and mysticism. Others tended toward a rationalism which almost completely ignored the work of the Spirit in the life. In the sixteenth century the Socinians declared that it was erroneous to believe that the persons of the Trinity possessed a single essence. In this teaching they echoed the Arians, but they went beyond them in denying the preexistence of the Son and defining the Holy Spirit as "a virtue or energy flowing from God to man."

From the Reformed church itself there arose the serious trouble in connection with what is known as Arminian theology

(Arminius, 1560-1609). The entire tendency of this teaching was to emphasize human effort and will, and to make salvation a work of man rather than a work of God, with the human will replacing the work of the Spirit in regeneration. The Synod of Dort (1618-19) met to deal with the matter, and it condemned Arminian theology, emphasizing in the strongest possible way the need of the working and power of the Holy Spirit. However, the synod did not erase Arminian theology, which flourishes to this day. The Puritan movement in England did much to counter Arminianism by its emphasis on the doctrine of grace.

C. John Owen (1616-1683)

One of the most important contributions of the Puritans was Owen's book *Discourse Concerning the Holy Spirit*. Many think his work has never been superseded. It is a development of the great Reformation principles in relation to the Holy Spirit and the Christian life, and its value cannot be estimated.

D. Abraham Kuyper (1837-1920)

The work of Kuyper is also a classic in its field, particularly in view of the rationalism which had swept over Europe. Swedenborg (1688-1722) denied the Trinity. Schleiermacher (1768-1834), though he countered the prevalent rationalism by emphasizing the need and reality of personal religion, denied the objective realities of the incarnation, the cross, and the coming of the Spirit. His doctrine of the Trinity was Sabellian—the persons of the Godhead were only modes of manifestation. The distinct personality of the Spirit was denied, and the Spirit's work was defined as "the collective Spirit of the new corporate life that was initiated by Christ." Ritschl (1822-1889) revived the Monarchianism of Paul of Samosata. His was a theology without metaphysics, which necessarily affected his view of the Spirit.

E. The Plymouth Brethren (1825)

It is to the Brethren that we owe a proper understanding of the baptizing work of the Spirit and the distinct nature of the New Testament church. The church owes much to their testimony to the importance of the Word of God, the illumination of the Spirit, and the position which the believer has in Christ by the work of the Spirit. There were deplorable schisms within their group, but theirs was a necessary witness to the presence, power, and guidance of the Spirit in the church.

F. Neoorthodoxy

Neoorthodoxy is a twentieth century movement arising out of the theology of Karl Barth (1886-   ). It was a reaction to the liberalism that held sway until the horrors of a world war forced men to think more seriously about sin and their own lack of competency to solve their own problems. The neoorthodox movement claimed to be a new reformation which called men back to the Bible. It did this, but not to the Bible of the Reformers, for neoorthodox theologians have willingly embraced the teachings of liberalism concerning the accuracy and truth of the Bible while at the same time trying to preach the message of the Bible.

Although neoorthodoxy has about as many exponents as there are neoorthodox theologians, it may be said that in general its view of the Holy Spirit leaves much to be desired. Most neoorthodox writers deny the distinct personality of the Spirit and affirm His deity only in that He is represented as a divine manifestation of God. The Holy Spirit is regarded as more of an activity of God than a person of the Godhead.

Barth's own view of the Trinity has been called modalistic, though he would reject the term. He rejects what is commonly conceived of as modalism of divine manifestation of God in three ways as saying too little in rightly expressing the doctrine of the Trinity. On the other hand, he rejects the term "person" in regard to the Trinity as teaching too much; i.e., tritheism or three Gods. His view seems to be that the Trinity is a threefold mode of manifestation and less than three persons. Barth, in contrast to most neoorthodox teachers, does believe in the deity of the Spirit.

G. Neoliberalism

The rise and wide acceptance of neoorthodox theology has caused liberalism to examine its own tenets. The result has been the new liberalism, which is the old liberalism with a tendency to take sin more seriously and to be less optimistic. Its approach to world problems may be different, but its teachings differ little from the older liberalism. The new liberal dispenses quickly and completely with the orthodox doctrine of the Spirit simply because he does not believe in the deity of the Second Person of the Trinity. Hence there is in reality no Trinity, and of course no divine Third Person. The Spirit is merely a function of God without possessing any distinct quality of personality.

H. Pentecostalism

Undoubtedly modern Pentecostalism is a reaction to the sterility that began to characterize the established churches in the modern era. It emphasizes the baptism of the Spirit as a second work of grace for enduement with power, and it promotes a return to experiencing all the gifts which were given and used in New Testament times. The orthodox doctrine concerning the person of the Spirit is assumed; it is the reality of the work of the Spirit in the lives of Christians that is promoted, and not always correctly.

Thus in the sweep of church history one sees first the formulation of what has come to be known as the orthodox doctrine of the Spirit, then the definition of it in the early councils, and the development of it during the Reformation. With every surge toward defining or developing the truth, there have been movements away from it, either in the form of rationalistic coldness or unbalanced enthusiasm and mysticism. History should teach us that orthodox doctrine is not only important to faith but equally vital to life. Perhaps in no doctrine is this wedding of truth and life more important than in the doctrine concerning the Holy Spirit.

HELPFUL BOOKS ON THE HOLY SPIRIT

There are many books on the doctrine of the Holy Spirit. Each fulfills different purposes. Anybody's list will be selective and influenced by what he himself has found particularly helpful. This list is no exception.

BARCLAY, WILLIAM. *The Promise of the Spirit.* Philadelphia: Westminster Press, 1960. Combines devotional emphasis with exegesis.

BARTH, KARL. *The Holy Ghost and the Christian Life.* London: Muller, 1938.

BIEDERWOLF, WILLIAM EDWARD. *A Help to the Study of the Holy Spirit,* 4th ed. New York: Fleming H. Revell Co., 1904. Contains an excellent bibliography.

CANDLISH, J. S. *The Work of the Holy Spirit.* Edinburgh: T. T. & T. Clark, 1883. Brief and lucid handbook.

CHAFER, LEWIS SPERRY. *He That Is Spiritual.* Chicago: Moody Press, 1943. Now distributed by Dunham Publishing Company. Careful distinctions, and exceedingly helpful on the spiritual life.

CUMMING, JAMES ELDER. *"Through the Eternal Spirit."* London: S. W. Partridge & Co., 1891. One of the standard works on pneumatology. Well organized.

DIXON, A. C., ed. *The Holy Spirit in Life and Service.* New York: Fleming H. Revell Co., 1895. Contains addresses by various men, including W. J. Erdman, A. J. Gordon, and A. T. Pierson.

DOWNER, ARTHUR CLEVELAND. *The Mission and Ministration of the Holy Spirit.* Edinburgh: T. T. & T. Clark, 1909. Comprehensive, well organized, and comparable to Kuyper.

HENDRY, GEORGE S. *The Holy Spirit in Christian Theology.* Philadelphia: Westminster Press, 1956. Neoorthodox.

KUYPER, ABRAHAM. *The Work of the Holy Spirit.* Grand Rapids: Wm. B. Eerdmans Publishing Co., 1900. A classic.

MARSH, F. E. *Emblems of the Holy Spirit.* New York: Alliance Press, 1911. Study of the typology of the Holy Spirit.

MORGAN, G. CAMPBELL. *The Spirit of God.* New York: Fleming H. Revell Co., 1900. One of his best.

121

MOULE, H. C. G. *Veni Creator: Thoughts on the Person and Work of the Holy Spirit of Promise.* London: Hodder & Stoughton, 1890. Excellent.

MURRAY, ANDREW. *The Spirit of Christ.* Grand Rapids: Zondervan Publishing House, reprint of 1888 edition. Meditations by this well-known writer and Dutch Reformed pastor.

OCKENGA, HAROLD J. *The Spirit of the Living God.* New York: Fleming H. Revell Co., 1947. High quality sermons.

OWEN, JOHN. *The Holy Spirit, His Gifts and Powers.* Grand Rapids: Kregel Publications, 1954. Kuyper regarded this as an unsurpassed classic.

PACHE, RENE. *The Person and Work of the Holy Spirit.* Chicago: Moody Press, 1954. Lucid, well-outlined, and particularly suited for personal study.

PIERSON, ARTHUR T. *The Acts of the Holy Spirit, Being an Examination of the Active Mission and Ministry of the Spirit of God, the Divine Paraclete, As Set Forth in the Acts of the Apostles.* New York: Fleming H. Revell Co., 1895.

RAMM, BERNARD. *The Witness of the Spirit; an Essay on the Contemporary Relevance of the Internal Witness of the Holy Spirit.* Grand Rapids: Wm. B. Eerdmans Publishing Co., 1959.

SANDERS, J. OSWALD. *The Holy Spirit of Promise; the Mission and Ministry of the Comforter.* Fort Washington, Pa.: Christian Literature Crusade, 1959.

SMEATON, GEORGE. *The Doctrine of the Holy Spirit.* Edinburgh: T. T. & T. Clark, 1889. Another classic in the field. Includes an historical survey of the doctrine.

SWETE, HENRY BARCLAY. *The Holy Spirit in the New Testament.* London: Macmillan Co., 1909.

THOMAS, W. H. GRIFFITH. *The Holy Spirit of God.* Grand Rapids: Wm. B. Eerdmans Publishing Co., 1955. Treats the doctrine biblically, historically, systematically, and practically. Very comprehensive.

TORREY, R. A. *The Holy Spirit: Who He Is and What He Does.* New York: Fleming H. Revell Co., 1927.

UNGER, MERRILL F. *The Baptizing Work of the Holy Spirit.* Wheaton: Scripture Press, 1953. Excellent treatment of this difficult aspect of the doctrine.

WALVOORD, JOHN F. *The Holy Spirit.* Grand Rapids: Dunham Publishing Company, 1958. A comprehensive textbook.

SUBJECT INDEX

Abelard, 116
Anointing, 45-46, 72-73
Apostleship, 85
Aquinas, Thomas, 116
Arianism, 112-13
Arminians, 117-18
Assurance, 106
Attributes, 17-18
Augustine, 114

Baptism
  of Christ, 45
  of Holy Spirit, 74-79
  of water, 74
Blasphemy against Holy Spirit, 13,
  52-53

Call, 61-62
Canon, 40
Chalcedon, Council of, 115
Christ
  and Holy Spirit, 45-48
  death of, 48-49
  resurrection of, 49-51
Christlikeness, 7, 101-2
Clothing, 25
Constantinople, Council of, 113-14
Convicting of Spirit, 20, 58-59
Creation, 30-32

Dedication, 95-97
Demons, 52-53
Discerning spirits, 90
Dort, Synod of, 118
Dove, 25

Earnest, 26
Elohim, 31
Emblem, 24
Ephesus, Council of, 114
Eschatology, 108-10
Evangelism, 89
Exhortation, 90

Faith, 64, 65, 90
Filling of Spirit
  and baptism, 75
  in Christ, 46-47
  in N. T., 93-103
  in O. T., 42

Fire, 26

Generation of Son, 21
Gifts
  general, 55-56
  spiritual, 83-92
Giving, 91
Grace
  common, 55-60
  efficacious, 61-63

Healing, 86-88

Illustration, meaning of, 24
Indwelling of Spirit
  in N. T., 67-73
  in O. T., 41-42
  permanence of, 70-71
Infants, regeneration of, 66
Inspiration
  author of, 35-36
  definition of, 33
  of N. T., 37-38
  verbal, 34
Intercession of Spirit, 13

Jehovah, 20

Kuyper, Abraham, 118

Leading of Spirit, 47, 97, 105

Millennium, 109-10
Ministering, 90
Miracles
  of Christ, 47-48
  spiritual gift of, 86-88
Montanism, 111-12
Moody, D. L., 75

Neoliberalism, 119
Neoorthodoxy, 119
New nature, 66
Nicea, Council of, 113, 114

Obedience, relation to indwelling,
  70
Oil, 27
O. T. quotations in N. T., 39-40
Owen, John, 118

123

SELECT SCRIPTURE INDEX

Passages on which interpretative comment is made in the text